JESUS OF NAZARETH

A NEW LOOK

JESUS OF NAZARETH
A NEW LOOK

Paul Baker, MBE, *Barrister*
A Reader (retd.) in the Church of England

JANUS PUBLISHING COMPANY
London, England

First published in Great Britain 1997
by Janus Publishing Company
Edinburgh House, 19 Nassau Street
London W1N 7RE

British Library Cataloguing-in-Publication Data.
A catalogue record for this book is available from the British Library.

ISBN 1 85756 312 3

Cover design Nick Eagleton

Photoset by Keyboard Services, Luton
Printed and bound in England by
Antony Rowe Ltd,
Chippenham, Wilts

Contents

v

Contents

Part 1

JESUS IN NAZARETH AND CAPERNAUM

A Study of the hidden Years

Introduction

Most Christians will want to know as much as possible about Jesus, the Founder of Christianity, and a multitude of books and articles have been written about Him. Immense resources in scholarship and theological study have been devoted to this subject and it must be a rash layman who ventures into this field. However, this vast literature is almost entirely concerned with the life of Jesus from when He began the ministry in Galilee until His last appearance on this earth or with the circumstances of His birth. Yet He must have lived for at least some 25 years with His family in Nazareth and it seems to me that an attempt ought to be made to explore what this might have been like. God the Father must surely have intended this period to be a preparation for the ministry and not just a wasted time while Jesus was growing up.

The current teaching of the Church that Jesus was God Incarnate does imply, however, that He needed no preparation and that the period before He began His ministry was no more than a time of waiting which can be safely ignored. The absence of information about it in the Gospels is then to be expected and any attempt to explore or study it would be wasted time.

On the other hand, if Jesus was born in the normal way as the first child of Joseph and Mary the situation is quite different and a period of preparation for His ministry would be appropriate. St Luke's Gospel tells us that Jesus grew in favour with God, which must indicate that there was a seriousness about this period of His life. It must indicate too that He increased in the Holy Spirit more and more, as we ourselves may hope to do throughout our lives. There seems to me to be very good evidence that Jesus was born and raised very much as we are ourselves, as I have endeavoured to show in the following pages. It may therefore be of great value to us to contemplate what kind of life Jesus may have led with His immediate family, as well as with their neighbours and the general community. As He was the only human being who could become the Son of God, every aspect of His life needs to be explored, even though conjecture must necessarily play a large part so far as this particular period is concerned. This is no doubt the reason why scholars eschew this part of the life of Jesus, there being no verifiable records on which they can rely. Nevertheless, there are echoes in the Gospels of this very important and formative period, as I shall try to show, and a study of it may be able to throw some light on the years of the public ministry.

Chapter One

The Birth of Jesus

The general view among scholars now seems to be that Jesus was born as the natural son of Joseph and Mary. This view arises because the birth narratives given by St Luke and the author of the gospel attributed to St Matthew cannot be taken as historical. The reasons for this are summarised below, but two points must be noted. First, the circumstances surrounding the birth as given in each of these narratives are very different and cannot be reconciled; secondly, they agree in only one particular, namely that Jesus was born in Bethlehem. Each writer goes to considerable lengths to show that Joseph was descended from the royal line of David and no doubt both he and Mary would have been very proud of that connection. It is not therefore in the least unlikely that they were both desirous that their first child should be born in Bethlehem, the City of David. Luke, who had the opportunity to talk to Mary and surely must have done so, would have learned from her that when the couple arrived in Bethlehem they found it difficult to obtain accommodation, which is not at all an unusual experience. The innkeeper may well have sent them to a neighbouring house where a crib for a baby was not to hand. As a portable manger could quite easily be adapted for the purpose, there is every reason to suppose that this was done. The basic tradition of the birth of Jesus in Bethlehem therefore stands, though the stories that have been weaved around it must be regarded as poetic embellishment. This must be particularly so in the imagery that has been built up around a birth in a stable, because of St Luke's reference to a manger. There is no mention of a stable in either Gospel. Nor is it likely that Joseph, a skilled craftsman, would have allowed his first child, a descendant from the royal line of David, to be born in such circumstances.

We may now turn to the question of the natural birth of Jesus.

The Gospel Accounts

St Matthew's Gospel. One of the principal objects of the author of this work was to demonstrate that the prophecies in the Old Testament which were thought to have any relation at all to the Messiah were in fact fulfilled in the life of Jesus. The splendid story of the Magi and King Herod seems to have evolved in response to those prophecies which expected a birth in Bethlehem as the City of David, a call out of Egypt and that the Messiah should be called a Nazarene. It is not conceivable that the events described in the story could have occurred without there being some echo of them at least in St Luke's Gospel, if not in other literature. The tribute which the story pays to Jesus is not in any way lessened, because it is imaginative and not historical, and it provides links with what subsequently happened.

St Luke's Gospel. Luke had been a diligent researcher for his Gospel and thought it essential to have an account of the birth of Jesus which would reflect His subsequent achievement. At the time he was writing, the only possible source of information he could have used would have been Mary, the Mother of Jesus. She must have revealed the link with her kinswoman Elizabeth, the mother of John the Baptist, and very likely explained how she and Joseph went with the Child to Jerusalem so that they could do everything prescribed in the law. Luke may well have seen the importance of emphasising the Davidic descent and the birth in Bethlehem. The events which he describes, though making an immensely valuable contribution to Christian literature, cannot be regarded as historical. They are a testimony to his belief that Jesus was a unique person and that His birth must have had unusual importance.

St Mark's Gospel. The fact that St Mark makes no reference to the birth of Jesus must mean that neither he nor any of those persons who could have aided him in composing the work thought that anything of an unusual nature had taken place. It seems very possible that St Mark's family were kinsmen or at least close friends of the family of Jesus. At any rate it is widely thought that the Last Supper took place in the upper room of the house in which St Mark lived, for he would not otherwise have been able to accompany Jesus and the disciples to the garden of Gethsemane. There is little doubt that he must have been 'the young man with nothing on but a linen cloth' and this would explain his presence in the narrative. He would therefore have been more likely to know about the birth and childhood of Jesus than the other evangelists.

Jesus the Son of God

The Christian Faith wholly depends upon the belief that Jesus is the unique Son of God, of one substance with the Father, and that this must be founded on His conception in the womb of His mother Mary by the Holy Spirit. At the same time it depends also upon the belief that Jesus was perfect Man, being of the substance of his mother. Yet it must surely be the case that perfect manhood requires the substance of a human father as well as a human mother. Jesus therefore must have had the substance of His father Joseph, by which He is of the House of David. At his birth Jesus began the long preparation for manhood during which, as He grew in grace, He took on also the substance of the Father. If that substance could have been imparted to Him in the womb it could also be imparted after his birth when He had achieved a human nature able to bear such a role. This interpretation avoids the difficulties that arise from a contemplation of an Infant being also God and the burden this would place upon Joseph and Mary. It explains the voice which spoke to Jesus at His baptism: 'Thou art my Son, my Beloved; on Thee my favour rests.' (Mark 1:11). It may be argued that the Holy Child, the only Son of God, would have been in the care of the angels and so made the burden to be borne by His earthly parents no greater than that of any parents. But in his temptations the Man Jesus rejected this very idea and, indeed, in practice, how could a boundary be drawn between the care required of the angels and that of His parents? Would the angels allow tears that might be normal to Joseph and Mary? The more one contemplates this situation, the more it shows itself to be impracticable and impossible to conceal, so that the world at large would have to be aware of it. Nor could the childhood and adolescence of such a person not have been recorded in all the gospels, let alone in secular history. The absence of any such records must surely be conclusive.

Jesus and the Holy Spirit

The Church, generally speaking, nevertheless believes that the Holy Spirit influenced the life of Jesus from the time of His conception, and this cannot be regarded as unreasonable. That the conception could have been by that Spirit is, to me, unthinkable as a biological fact and the credal statements to that effect can only be accepted under protest as representing a form of words covering the general belief already stated. The appearance of these statements in the birth stories already noted can only be explained as later additions to the text at a time when the pagan world of the Roman Empire expected the divinity of an earthly person, eg the Emperor, to have arisen from a virginal conception occasioned by one of the pantheon of gods. As Christianity became more widely spread through the Roman Empire it may have been thought appropriate to elaborate the birth stories so as to provide for this in the case of Jesus. It does not now seem to be either necessary or appropriate to continue to make such a claim, and arguments against it are further examined in the next chapter. Indeed it may be that it has now begun to be harmful to do so in the context of the credal statements which also contain unquestioned historical fact, such as that Jesus 'suffered under Pontius Pilate'. That the Church believes in the mystery of the Trinity is unquestioned, but questions must and do arise about the Virgin Birth and so cause difficulty to many people. Moreover, the pattern of morning worship in the Anglican Church has changed from Morning Prayer to Parish Communion with the introduction of the *Alternative Service Book*. While the latter has been widely and rightly acclaimed, the change has given a new prominence to the Nicene Creed. This, in comparison with the much shorter and easily remembered Apostles' Creed, has the following defects: it is very wordy, in striking contrast to the Lord's Prayer for instance. It strongly asserts belief in the Virgin Birth and totally ignores any belief in the humanity of Jesus, a defect which the now forgotten Athanasian Creed was intended to correct. It ascribes a masculine gender to the Holy Spirit, which is quite unnecessary and which the version in the *Book of Common Prayer* does not do.

The only justification for the continued use of the Nicene Creed is that it is very ancient, though it is not as ancient as the Apostles' Creed, and therefore, in spite of its obvious defects, gains in esteem the longer it is used. The Christian Church ought to be able to do better than this! A summary of Christian doctrine written by Irenaeus about AD 180 closely resembles the Apostles' Creed. He speaks of the Church as

'believing in one God the Father Almighty, who made

heaven and earth, the sea and all that in them is, and in one Christ Jesus, the Son of God, who was incarnate for our salvation, and in the Holy Ghost, who by the prophets proclaimed the dispensations and advents of our dear Lord Christ Jesus and His birth of a virgin and His suffering and His Resurrection from the dead and His Ascension in the flesh into heaven and His coming from heaven in the glory of the Father to sum up all things and to raise up all flesh of the whole human race'.

This also shows no trace of conception by the Holy Spirit, indicates only the purity of the Virgin Mary and establishes that Jesus was her first-born Child.

While considering this subject, it is worth noting that the translators of the *New English Bible*, New Testament scholars and Christian theologians have all been aware, probably for most of this century, that the Virgin Birth cannot be proved from the Gospel accounts. Because a denial of it is thought to strike at the very foundations of the Christian faith, no attempt has been made to do so. On the other hand, the commission responsible for the *Report on Doctrine in the Church of England*, which was first published in 1938, stated (page 82):

'There are some among us who hold that a full belief in the historical Incarnation is more consistent with the supposition that our Lord's birth took place under the normal conditions of human generation. In their minds the notion of a Virgin Birth tends to mar the complete-ness of the belief that in the Incarnation God revealed Himself at every point in and through human nature.'

The Gospels show that the Holy Spirit did not come upon Jesus in full measure in His mother's womb but increased in Him more and more during the period of His preparation for the Ministry until His total obedience to the Will of God was

8

made clear at His baptism. The notion of the Virgin Birth is not only not fundamental but is probably both a harmful and heretical doctrine. It is therefore high time that it was described as such.

Chapter Two

The Birth Story Examined

If the material relating to the Virgin Birth is in fact a later insertion in the birth stories in St Matthew and St Luke, its deletion would leave a connected narrative in each case. The following extracts demonstrate that this is so.

St Matthew

The opening verses record the descent of Jesus, son of David, concluding with 'Joseph, the husband of Mary, who gave birth to Jesus called Messiah' The *New English Bible* has a footnote that one early witness has 'Joseph, to whom Mary, a virgin, was betrothed, was the father of Jesus called Messiah.' In those times, to be the husband of and to be betrothed to had the same meaning, so that the Gospel has already made a very positive statement about the birth of Jesus. Verses 18 to 25 are then omitted as being the added material and the narrative continues with Chapter 2: 'Jesus was born at Bethlehem in Judea...', and there is no observable break.

The additional material, however, begins with the phrase: 'This is the story of the birth of the Messiah...' and is quite obviously an alternative account of the birth which can only be explained as a later insertion.

10

Jesus in Nazareth and Capernaum

St Luke

The account of the birth of Jesus given in this Gospel is already full of heavenly activity in fulfilment of St Luke's wholly understandable desire to show that so unique a person must have had a special kind of birth. Only a minor adjustment would therefore be needed to account for the Virgin Birth, but it might be thought that a very odd way was chosen to do this. The additional material in this case is inserted in the annunciation speech of the angel Gabriel, who, as he is proclaiming the majesty of Jesus and has already announced that 'he will bear the title "Son of the Most High"' is rather rudely interrupted by Mary. 'How can this be,' she says, 'when I have no husband?' The angel answers, 'The Holy Spirit will come upon you and the power of the Most High will overshadow you; and for this reason the holy child to be born will be called "Son of God".' It would be very unusual for an angel's message to be interrupted in this way, particularly to make him contradict himself in so important a particular as the title to be borne by the holy child. For this reason alone the interruption must be regarded as a later insertion.

St Luke also traces the descent of Jesus, though at a later point in his Gospel and in the reverse order to that of St Matthew. In Chapter 3, at verse 23, he records that: 'When Jesus began his work he was about thirty years old, the son, as people thought, of Joseph.'

The inclusion of the words 'as people thought' would make irrelevant the whole attempt to trace the descent of Jesus, since if He was not the son of Joseph he could not then be the son of David. St Luke would not therefore have written those words and they must be regarded as inserted by a later hand.

St John

There is a curious verse in the prologue to this gospel which

11

appears to be a later insertion, namely verse 13. The previous verse affirms that, to all who did receive Jesus and yielded Him their allegiance, 'he gave the right to become children of God.' Verse 13 then adds 'not born of any human stock, or by the fleshly desire of a human father, but the offspring of God himself.' These words are clearly intended to refer to Jesus, but they do not say so and can therefore only mean the immediately preceding persons, namely those who receive Jesus, who most certainly will be those born of human stock. It can only be assumed that this verse too is a later addition and, like those in the other two Gospels, not very well done.

St Mark

There are of course no references either to the birth or the childhood of Jesus in this Gospel. It is of interest to note however that a very early addition seems to have been made to its text. Professor C. H. Dodd, the supreme translator of the *New English Bible*, in his book *Parables of the Kingdom*, has drawn attention to the passage in 4:11–20, in which the parable of the Sower is converted into an allegory, though in a confused way. He says the passage is strikingly unlike other sayings of Jesus and has a vocabulary characteristic of the apostolic writers of the early Church. He therefore concludes that this is 'not a part of the primitive tradition of the words of Jesus, but a piece of apostolic teaching.' We may suppose it would have been inserted at this point much later on, and in a similar way to the additions to the other gospels noted above, and really also not very well done.

The Changes – How and When Made

The next questions that arise are when and how such changes could be made. As to the former, it could not have been before AD 180 as the quotation from Irenaeus in Chapter One has established. The most likely time would have been mid-third century, when the church was growing rapidly within the Roman Empire and the need to prove the divinity of Jesus

to a pagan world would have been of the greatest importance. Certainly by the end of that century the Gospel had
reached England in sufficient force to persuade Constantine
to launch his bid for the imperial purple under the banner of
the Cross and bring it to a successful conclusion. Such
changes could only have been made at a time when there
would have been relatively few manuscripts of the Gospels
extant and the central control of the Church from Rome
universally acknowledged. All such manuscripts could have
been called in for verification, but would in fact have had to
be destroyed. What would then have seemed quite innocuous
amendments would have been incorporated in newly written
copies and perhaps a wider distribution of the new manuscripts effected. Such a procedure would account for the
absence of any copies of the Gospels earlier than the fourth
century in so far as these can be dated.

Chapter Three

A Visit to Jerusalem

To what extent Jesus was guided by the Holy Spirit during His life in Nazareth we cannot know, but St Luke tells that 'the child grew big and strong and full of wisdom and God's favour was upon Him'. That would most certainly accord with the general belief of the Church and gives good support to the story of the visit to Jerusalem which follows next in St Luke's gospel. We may note at this point, however, that at the conclusion of the story the Evangelist repeats the same point in a different way: 'as Jesus grew up He advanced in wisdom and in favour with God and men.' To advance is to move from the less to the more, and in Jesus this would indicate a normal growth through childhood and adolescence and so emphasise that His life in Nazareth could be a preparation for the ministry to come.

The Journey
Verses 41 to 52 of the second chapter of St Luke's Gospel throw so much light on the life in Nazareth that it is worth considering them in close detail. To go every year to the Passover festival would have been quite expensive in terms of time and money spent, and therefore of income lost. Joseph

was a carpenter, most probably what would now be described as a small business man. He may have had hired servants who could continue some form of service to his customers, but his absence must have taken its toll on the finances of the business. That absence would most likely have been about three weeks, allowing six or seven days for the journey each way in a caravan that could only move at the speed of the slowest member and which obviously included children. To be able to go every year must imply a fair degree of prosperity for the business and the family, which, by this time, would have included seven or eight children. St Mark has listed the brothers of Jesus as James, Joseph, Judas and Simon and refers to His sisters. (6:3). There is no reason to suppose that they did not all accompany the party, thereby giving rise to the circumstance that Jesus was not missed when He remained behind in Jerusalem.

This must have come about in the first place because the children would have been accommodated with various friends and relations, for they could not all have been under one roof. This surely is where the link with the parents of St Mark must have begun and which led on to the most likely use of the upper room in their house for the Last Supper which Jesus took with His disciples. Having reached the age of 12, Jesus could have been, indeed clearly was, left to His own devices, while His parents kept a closer eye on the younger children. So, and unbeknown to His parents, He joined the teachers in the Temple and demonstrated the exceptional wisdom and intelligence which so amazed all who heard Him.

The Temple
The Temple precincts at that time comprised the great platform built by Herod the Great, most of which still exists. The southern half comprised the Court of the Gentiles and was, as its name implies, open for public access. On the east side were the Porch of Solomon and the Beautiful Gate, giving access to the Mount of Olives, and on the west was the gate to the city.

Under an arcade of Corinthian columns at the south side were the tables of the money changers and the stalls of the sellers of doves and animals for ritual sacrifices. A low wall separated this Court from the northern half of the platform, itself in two parts. To the east was the Court of Women, to which no Gentiles could be admitted and which gave access to the Temple structure on the north-western part of the platform through a succession of open spaces, steps and balustrades. Only males could enter this part, worshippers to prepare their sacrifices in the Court of Israel and the priests to have access to the Temple building. In the Court of Women was the Treasury and in its northern and eastern arcades would be found the teachers and doctors of the Law who were apparently in regular session there.

At the conclusion of the festival the family joins the caravan for the return home with the children, apparently scattered amongst their parents, friends and relations. There now follows an incident which is so real and so much like what can happen in any family that it must have come directly from Mary herself and so gives exceptional value to the whole account. After a day's journey Joseph and Mary find out that Jesus is missing and with great anxiety return to Jerusalem, leaving the other children in the care of friends and relations for the rest of the journey home. On arrival at the city nobody knows where Jesus is and His parents seem to have no idea where to look for Him. We are immediately made aware that they had no inkling that Jesus was in any way different from their other children for if they had known they would surely not have lost sight of Him as they did, nor been as unaware of His interests, as they evidently were.

The Search for Jesus
After three days, or at any rate rather longer than it took them to return to the city, they find Jesus 'sitting in the temple surrounded by the teachers, listening to them and putting questions.' At this point we have to remember that Jesus had

been in Jerusalem for a week or more and had presumably spent a lot of that time in the Temple, where He must have been recognised as a quite exceptionally gifted child. He must have come to know some of those teachers quite well and would have been able to renew acquaintance with them in subsequent years, for there is no reason to suppose that Joseph and Mary would have abandoned their regular annual visits as a result of this mishap.

'They found Him.' Most parents will have experienced not being able to find a child from whom they have become separated for whatever reason. The anxiety which immediately grips them is acute and is accompanied by countless fears as their search is prolonged. We do not know what prompted Joseph and Mary eventually to go to the Temple; perhaps it was to pray for guidance, but their relief at finding Jesus there can well be imagined. An understandable feeling of anger must have come into their minds. We can therefore fully understand the reproach in Mary's voice when she says 'My son, why have you treated us like this?' Why indeed! Jesus was enjoying a new freedom because He had reached the age at which boys could begin a preparation for manhood. As recently as at the end of the 19th century in England, a boy would leave school at 12 in order to begin to learn his father's business, as did my own father . So Jesus was happy to go on His own to the Temple and quite forgot to tell His parents what He was doing. He might have been lodging with someone near the Temple who was not in regular touch with the Nazareth party and did not know they had set out for home. Some such reason must have explained why Jesus had lost contact with His parents and not realised how anxious they might be when they missed Him.

The Outcome

There can be no doubt that the exclamations which St Luke has attributed to Mary must be very close to if not her actual words to Jesus. The reply made by Him is much more likely to have been the question which St Luke addressed to Mary: 'What made you search? Did you not know that He would be in the Temple?' I believe that Jesus would have been covered with confusion at being reunited with His parents in this way and, in her joy at finding Him, Mary would not remember what He said but only that He did what any child would do and embraced His mother to comfort her. That indeed would be one of the things which she 'treasured up in her heart'. St Luke must have found this episode difficult to fit into his Gospel, as he considered the Person whom Jesus became. So he attributes words to Jesus to justify His behaviour which are not at all becoming in His mouth and I am confident are not what Jesus would have said. They are, however, perfectly proper questions for St Luke to ask of Mary and she clearly could not answer them. This artless story can only confirm that neither Mary nor Joseph had any inkling of a special destiny for their eldest son and that nothing had been revealed to them at His birth.

It may be noted that the earlier translation of this question – 'Wist ye not that I must be about my Father's business?' – would have indicated that Jesus was aware of His future mission, whereas the modern translation does not attribute such knowledge to Him at this stage. The question as to when Jesus did become aware of it cannot be answered for certain, but may well not have been until He was in His mid-twenties. St Luke's conclusion to the story is entirely apt: Jesus returned with His parents to Nazareth and 'continued to be under their authority', because of course He had surrendered Himself to them in the Temple. That He then advanced has already been noted, and we may reflect that an advance can only occur where it is needed and that the Holy Spirit still had work to do.

Chapter Four

Jesus at Work

The Carpenter

The business of a carpenter is one which can have a special interest for any boy and perhaps particularly so for one who is exceptionally gifted. There is first of all the correct use of the available tools and the possibility for an inventive mind to fashion tools to suit particular requirements. W. L. Goodman, in his *History of Woodworking Tools*, reckons there would have been 14 different types of tool available to the carpenter in the Greek and Roman period. These would have included axes, chisels, drills, smoothing and other types of plane, with knives and rules which would have enabled a high standard of craftsmanship to be achieved. All of these would be easily recognisable today, though they would have refinements in design and substitute steel for bronze or iron. The complete range and quality of these tools was most likely to have been found in the major cities, but Jerusalem had buildings such as Herod the Great's magnificent Temple, the Roman fortress and palace, Antonia, the High Priest's house, and so on, which would have called for excellence in many crafts. Joseph would surely have had friends among the carpenters and joiners there who would have helped him to equip his workshop with a good selection of such tools. The townspeople of Nazareth and its neighbourhood were likely to have had access to a very good standard of work in this field, as well as the benefit of unusual skill in the family of Jesus.

Care is needed in the selection of the best timber for a given job, in marking it out so that it is cut to the best advantage and the right dimensions. It may be necessary to make a diagram to show how pieces of timber are to fit together, and this is often necessary in the learning process. Jesus would have been as diligent in mastering these techniques as in the study of the Torah. Then, as His younger brothers entered the workshop, they would need to be instructed – and what better teacher could they have had than Jesus himself? It must surely have been a very happy workshop indeed.

Given that Joseph would already have established or inherited a fairly prosperous business, probably able to employ some hired men, the arrival of his sons, who would surely have joined him, must have enlarged its scope, increased its turnover and improved profitability. It is therefore worth considering what the scope of such a business might have been. To do so it is necessary to make an assessment of contemporary Galilee around AD 15 to 25.

Galilee – The Local Scene

In his book *Galilee from Alexander the Great to Hadrian*, Sean Freyne describes how the territory forms a broad circle, with the Lake or Sea of Galilee at the mid-point on the east side, Lake Huleh the northern limit, Nairn marking the southern border and the western formed by the hill country and excluding the coastal plain. The whole area is fertile and produced all the important agricultural items that were in demand in the ancient world. The population was mainly agricultural, living in those close ties of kinship which would have facilitated the regular visits to Jerusalem made by

Jesus in Nazareth and Capernaum

Joseph and Mary and their family. Though separated from Judea by the Samaritans, Galilee retained its Jewishness and its connections with Jerusalem and the Temple worship. This situation had been consolidated under Herod the Great and a period of substantial peace and stability continued under his son Herod Antipas, whose combined rule extended from 47 BC to AD 39. The agricultural prosperity which characterised Galilee enabled it to support numerous cities and sizeable village settlements, with populations of the order of 15,000 not at all unusual. Many of these would have had walled fortifications, contributing to the general air of firm government and economic stability.

The most commonly spoken language was Aramaic, though for purposes of trade Greek was in general use as a *lingua franca* throughout Galilee. The large Jewish element would also use Hebrew on formal occasions and in the practice of their religion. Social stability was enhanced by the substantial number of small landowners, this being in accord with Roman policy, though there were also a number of tenant farmers and absentee landlords. There was a local upper class of petty nobles and men of substance centred on Herod's court at Tiberias – the Herodians of the Gospels. This situation is closely reflected in the parables of Jesus. As Roman currency was in general use it allowed an easy flow of trade and commerce, imports and exports, with all the surrounding territories and as far afield as Egypt and the Eastern Mediterranean countries. The town dwellers and the rural population had to bear a substantial weight of taxation, raised from land taxes, market tolls and customs duties, for the benefit of Herod Antipas and for the Roman tribute. In addition, the loyal Jew would pay a religious tithe which was very generally supported. These commitments were seen as acceptable because of the peaceful conditions which the long reign of Herod Antipas secured. The synagogue was the religious centre, whose ruler would be locally influential. The Council of the synagogue would be called upon to settle local arguments and often had power to inflict corporal punishment.

The relative peace of Galilee did not continue beyond the middle of the first century. The destruction caused by successive wars left no archaeological remains that can illuminate the people and the culture of the time of Jesus. Nevertheless, the surviving masonry and stonework indicate the existence of high standards of skill and craftsmanship, which would not have been confined to the work of masons. It is reasonable to assume that equal standards were to be found in the other crafts and particularly amongst the workers in wood. The tools that produced fine stonework, though few have survived from that period, would have had their equal in those available for woodwork, whose products were even less likely to endure. It can therefore be assumed with confidence that the carpentry business into which Jesus entered was one which had adequate tools and a high degree of craftsmanship. There would have been a good supply of both hardwood and softwood, the equal perhaps of the renowned cedars of Lebanon down to the humble pine.

The Family Business

On this basis it can be expected that Joseph and his workmen would have been able to produce a wide variety of artefacts to suit the needs of an urban as well as a rural population. In addition, carpentry is a leading craft in the design and construction of domestic buildings, so that Joseph may well have been rightly described as a carpenter and builder. It is recorded in Samuel 2:5 that 'carpenters and stonemasons built David a house'. We have already seen that his business must have been quite prosperous and from the technical point of view there is no reason to doubt this. So we may expect that in Nazareth two-storey dwellings would not have been uncommon and Joseph's own home might well have been of this kind. Near to it would have been a workshop with storage facilities, work benches and tool racks. We may suppose that, before Jesus and His brothers could enter the business, Joseph may well have employed men to assist him, for every craftsman needs a mate. An assistant to man the workshop might also have been required, whose duties could well have included the giving of instruction and help to the boys, who would surely have found the workshop a fascinating place, as boys still do, before they were old enough to join their father.

A carpenter is usually also described as a joiner, for wood is extensively used to make household fittings and furniture, and lighter articles than are involved in carpentry. The craft can extend into creative woodwork of all kinds, and the local hardwoods give many opportunities for useful and attractive items. This kind of work would undoubtedly have brought the family into touch with a large range of customers and employers both in Nazareth and in the surrounding villages. An echo of this can be found in St John's account of the wedding at Cana, for Jesus would hardly have been invited to it at so early a point in His ministry unless there had been some earlier connection. Thus this most useful and supportive activity would have made the family well known within the area in which it effectively operated.

Chapter Five

Family and Synagogue

The Family of Joseph and Mary

That the business which Joseph operated and managed was successful and reasonably prosperous is evidenced by the size of the family. As a member of the House of David, perhaps also entitled to be called a Son of David, he must have had some standing in the community in Nazareth, a responsible and respected man – a man of principle, according to St Matthew. Mary, through her kinswoman Elizabeth, was related to Zechariah, a priest from the uplands of Judea. These two would not have had so large a family, five boys and at least two girls, perhaps more, unless they were confident of their ability to care for them, house, clothe and feed them in a manner suitable to their own standing. Since Joseph's business would enable him to provide and equip a dwelling which could accommodate them all, we can expect that the family would have been able to live in comparative comfort.

These circumstances seem to me to imply that the children would have been well brought up and given the best education that was available, almost certainly from the synagogue.

Jesus in Nazareth and Capernaum

As an exceptionally gifted child, Jesus clearly profited from this as His encounter with the teachers in the Temple in Jerusalem demonstrates. But James, the eldest, as it is thought, of the other four boys, became the President of the Christian Church in Jerusalem, so he too must have had an education that could fit him for such a task. So I think we can justly assume that all the children were at least as well educated as any of their contemporaries. It would therefore seem most unlikely that the family was in any way impoverished or semi-literate, as some seem to suppose. It is much more likely that Jesus had an enjoyable and stimulating youth and adolescence in the midst of such a family and their relations and friends. For the members of the family the presence of such a person as Jesus would also have been a quite exceptional experience. The younger children, and there would be some in their infancy when Jesus was in His later teens, would find an elder brother very responsive to their needs. The older ones would likewise have enjoyed a special relationship not only with Him but also with one another because of His presence, exceptional gifts and general charisma. His parents, too, must have marvelled more and more at the delight of having such a child, even if only little as yet of the glory which was to come was made known to them. The wider family of relations, friends and neighbours could not have been unaware of an unusual young man in their midst and seen Him as a natural leader among their own children. In every generation the Jewish people have not lacked men and women of outstanding gifts in art and music, in poetry and drama, indeed in all forms of expression, and the community in Nazareth might well have wondered what was developing in their midst.

The Synagogue in Nazareth

In Nazareth the synagogue was the centre of the Jewish community and must have played a most important part in preparing Jesus for His future ministry. It is perfectly clear from the Gospels that Jesus and His whole family were regular adherents and it is more than likely that Joseph, as a descendant of David, would have been expected to hold a leading place. The exceptional qualities displayed by Jesus would have been very clear to the Rabbi and all the leading members of the congregation and there is no reason to suppose that they would do other than welcome such a member. It can be imagined that the Rabbi would have found Jesus a delightful member of his congregation from His childhood onwards. Jesus was bound to have been prominent in the school which would have met there. At first it would have been as an exceptionally gifted pupil, as evidenced by the account of the visit to Jerusalem when Jesus was 12, which St Luke has given. Such children are often difficult to manage, but that story makes a point of affirming that Jesus was obedient to His parents and He would surely have been equally subject to all in authority, but able in His special way to deal with any who lacked good sense or were hypocritical. As He grew to manhood His superior intelligence and charm of manner must have made Him a natural leader among those younger than Himself and in the whole community. So He would have been loved and respected by all who knew Him and would in due course have taken an honoured place in the congregation and doubtless in the community at large. This would have given him many opportunities for developing skills in public speaking and preaching from the texts of the Torah. He would have been proficient in the synagogue worship and the singing of psalms and hymns, which clearly formed a part of His later daily life with His disciples. The presence of such an unusual person there, as it became known outside Nazareth, might well have given Jesus a welcome reception in the neighbouring villages, perhaps as a representative of the synagogue, very likely as a member of the well-known family of carpenters and builders.

The Hierarchy in Jerusalem

We have already considered the implications of the visit to Jerusalem when Jesus was 12, and noted that the regularity of these visits, for there is no reason to suppose that they ceased thereafter, is evidence of the continuing prosperity of the family. Such regular contacts would indicate an ever widening circle of friends in the City, the existence of which has already been inferred from St Luke's account. Moreover it is hardly to be supposed that Jesus never again met the teachers in the Temple, but rather that He would have renewed acquaintance with them each year. These visits would be rather like a summer school and might have permitted Jesus to meet other visitors wishing to hear the teaching available in the Temple. In this way the reputation of this extraordinary young man might have begun to spread among the Jews of Judea as well as of Galilee. The interest which Jerusalem had for Jesus would not have been confined to the Temple, for surely His family would have wanted Him to visit friends in the City as well as in the surrounding villages, such as Bethany or Emmaus. He would most probably also have visited Jericho and learned of the dangers of the road. It cannot be supposed that when Jesus came to Jerusalem during His ministry that He was a stranger there. It might well have been that some of the men He later chose as His disciples had first made His acquaintance when they too were pilgrims in Jerusalem and recognised Him as a quite exceptional person.

It must also have been the case that Jesus would have become familiar with the religious practices of the Pharisees there and the role of the scribes, for He could only have gained such an intimate knowledge of them in Jerusalem. In these years also there may have been those among the religious establishment who sympathised with the views expressed by Jesus, such as Gamaliel, Nicodemus and Joseph of Arimathaea. The few occasions on which Jesus visited

27

Jerusalem during His ministry would not have sufficed for Him to know the situation there as well as He did, or to have found such support among those influential members of the Jewish Establishment. Other members of the Jewish ruling class may well have resented the emergence from despised Nazareth of so attractive a figure as Jesus. Before He began His ministry He might already have made them aware of the criticisms which were later developed so strongly, so that when He began to preach in Galilee emissaries were sent from Jerusalem to watch Him. He might have become a quite well-known visitor to the Temple and perhaps to the City during the Passover festivals each year, but it is most unlikely that any opposition He then aroused would have been any greater than that which existed between the various religious sects of the Jews. It might, however, account for the immediate hostility which Jesus encountered from Jerusalem as soon as He began the ministry, as is particularly noted by St Mark. On the other hand, St Luke (13:32) records that some Pharisees, who must have been from the Jerusalem delegation, came to Jesus to warn Him to leave Galilee because Herod Antipas was out to kill Him, so that even in this group there were those who supported Him.

Having, as it were, reached a degree of equality with the hierarchy in Jerusalem in terms of intelligence and judgment, it could have been that Jesus was entitled to wear some kind of distinguishing emblem or clothing which gave Him access to the Temple and led to His general recognition as a teacher or rabbi. It may be noted in this connection that some of those who sought healing from Him wished but to touch the tassel of His outer garment. Some similar robe might have been worn by the doctors of the law, the scribes and all those who were later always able to secure places near to Jesus and question and argue with Him.

The Pressures in Nazareth

There is no way of knowing for certain when Joseph, the

28

earthly Father of Jesus, died, but it may well have been the event which subsequently caused Jesus to leave Nazareth. It might well be reasonable to place it about two years or so before that took place. Until then it must be supposed that Jesus would have been Joseph's right hand man in the family business, assuming, as we must, that He continued in it. By now in His mid-twenties, Jesus would have attained a dignity and status in his own right commensurate with the standing accorded to him in Jerusalem, in the synagogue in Nazareth as well as in the business world there. With the death of Joseph, Jesus becomes the head of the family in every way. It is worth considering what this may have meant in terms of the pressures it would have lain upon Jesus at the time when He would be considering whether He must not now be about the business of His heavenly Father.

It is not at all unlikely that the four brothers of Jesus would be engaged in the business either as craftsmen in the carpenters' workshop or working on site in construction or maintenance work. In addition there would almost certainly have been hired men to assist them or work with them. A business operating on a fairly modest scale with 20 or so men would need careful management and it cannot be supposed that any enterprise with which Jesus was associated would receive anything less. The inference must therefore be that this business is likely to have operated on something more than a modest scale, simply because of the high standards it would have maintained in every department. It would surely have been popular in the community at large, and inevitably quite prosperous, so that the members of the family were generous supporters of good causes and thus individually well liked. How much more must this have applied to Jesus Himself. Within a short time of the death of Joseph, He is becoming more and more involved in all these aspects, quite apart from the leading place He already has in the synagogue and the annual pilgrimage to Jerusalem at the Passover festival. It is becoming perfectly clear that the only way in which He can conduct any mission such as that which is now occupying His mind is by making a complete break with all his connections in Nazareth. That this would be both difficult and painful is abundantly obvious, and a careful preparation would be needed for it, the more so because the precise nature of the mission He wished to undertake could not be revealed at this stage.

Chapter Six

The Break with Nazareth

The Separation

We may gain some idea of what this may have entailed by considering the parable of the prodigal son. The latter had first to explain why he wanted to leave a comfortable home to seek his fortune in another country. It is pretty clear that he did not have the sympathy of his brother, who could very well represent a larger family. The prodigal insists that he must go, a division of the inheritance is made, he departs and the parable then ceases to be relevant to this particular issue. Jesus almost certainly was unable to convince His family, His colleagues in the synagogue, His friends and neighbours or His business associates that it could possibly be right for Him, on the threshold of a successful career, to throw it all up in favour of some vague religious aspiration. It is not in the least difficult to imagine the situation! Jesus, however, is adamant and, being the person He is, the break is arranged with the minimum of rancour. It is hardly likely that Jesus would have been allowed to depart completely penniless and so some division of the family's assets, if not already made, would now have been allocated to Him. The whole experience may well have inspired the parable.

Jesus Moves to Capernaum

The Gospel accounts of the beginning of the ministry of Jesus make it clear that, on leaving Nazareth, He first established Himself in Capernaum, and appears to have acquired a house there, though He did not begin to preach until 'after John (the Baptist) had been arrested', according to Mark 1:14. There must therefore have been a quite lengthy interval, towards the end of which Jesus was baptised by John and subsequently withdrew into a desert place to wrestle with the temptations described by Matthew and Luke. In Mark 2:1, after the commencement of the ministry, we read that 'when He returned to Capernaum, the news went round that He was at home.' It is suggested that Jesus might have been staying at the house of Simon Peter, after healing his wife of a fever. But if Jesus was in Capernaum before He began the ministry, and though He may have known the fishermen before He left Nazareth, the word 'home' without any other indication is just as likely to mean that He had acquired His own house, perhaps by renting it, and was living alone there in retreat from the pressures of His former life in Nazareth. This view could be held to be supported by the reference in Matthew 9:1 that He 'came to His own town', which must be Capernaum and could as well be described as His home town at that time. Again there is the reference in Mark 7:24 to Jesus finding a house to stay in when He visited the territory of Tyre. Here He was in Gentile country, where 'He would have liked to remain unrecognised' and so would obviously have rented accommodation so as not to draw attention to Himself. If at this later stage in the ministry Jesus had funds to enable Him to do this, He would equally have been able to buy or rent a house on first arriving in Capernaum. That Jesus and His disciples did have funds at their disposal is evident from the Gospels and the selection of Judas Iscariot 'to carry the bag'.

On leaving Nazareth, Jesus would surely have required a period during which He could lay aside all those affairs which had pressed so heavily upon Him there. He would need to reconcile Himself to the break with His family. In his commentary on Mark, C. F. D. Moule observes in regard to 3:21 'it must have been unspeakably costly to both Him and His mother' and that both she and His brothers 'failed at this stage to understand Him'. So Jesus would be thinking about them and praying for them, though it was some considerable time before they realised that Jesus could no longer be tied to them.

Preparation for Ministry

Active preparation for the ministry would now need to be made and the selection of those who were to become His disciples must have occupied a considerable part of His thoughts and prayers. He could and surely would have used this quiet time in Capernaum to make contact, even perhaps close contact, with men whose character appealed to Him. It is not unlikely that He would already have met the fishermen, either as customers for repairs to their boats or as friends with whom He enjoyed a fishing trip when He could take time off from business. He might well have had dealings with Matthew (or Levi) the tax collector in the course of business, but even if not He would now have the opportunity to observe him at work and note that he behaved fairly in his difficult role. These five were from His own town and from them He chose His three closest friends, so it is very likely that a great deal of care would have gone into His choice of them.

There were also questions regarding the nature of the ministry that would need to be decided, such as His mission being primarily to the Jews and particularly to those who were being confused and misled by the scribes and Pharisees, the doctors of the law. Jesus would also have been observing and listening to John the Baptist, surely indeed meeting and talking with him and so convincing John that here was indeed someone who was greater than he.

That this interval between first arriving in Capernaum and the beginning of the ministry in Galilee could have been quite lengthy is confirmed in St John's Gospel. Here the writer is recording the recollections and meditations of the apostle and these often become confused. Moreover the apostle attaches signs to quite ordinary events so that they become extra-ordinary. Nevertheless an underlying layer of fact clearly exists, and can be used as historical data to supplement the synoptic writers, none of whom were apostles.

The first such event confirms an early link between Jesus and John the Baptist and, though the account of this (1:29–34) is used to express the latter's witness to One greater than he, it does not report an actual baptism, which may well have come later. Thus the incident is used as a sign in which the testimony of the Baptist is what matters and not the baptism itself, though the former is a much more positive statement than appears in the synoptics. Next, Jesus makes the acquaintance of some of the men who are to become his disciples, but to none of them does He say 'follow me'. Rather is this an opportunity for the apostle to show what an acute and deep perception of the people He met Jesus had, so that those who responded to him would say, as Nathanael did, 'Rabbi, you are the Son of God'. This should also be regarded as another sign and cannot replace the much more likely historical account in St Mark of the actual calling of the disciples.

The Wedding at Cana
There now follows the famous account of the wedding at Cana, which the apostle declares he has used as a sign. There can be no doubt that there was a wedding, but no one else saw in it what was revealed to St John and so it gains no other mention. Indeed, the keynote of the event may well have been

the comment which Jesus made to his mother, 'My time has not yet come'. The fascinating thing is that Jesus here met up with his mother again, and most probably with the other members of the family. This is because in 2:12 the apostle states, 'After this (the wedding) he went down to Capernaum in company with his mother, his brothers and his disciples, but they did not stay there long'. In effect they would have been there long enough to see that Jesus was comfortably lodged, as I am sure any mother would have wished to do, and that He seemed to be among friends. This is in striking contrast to the visit referred to in Mark 3:21, which His family made to Galilee soon after Jesus had appointed the Twelve. 'When His family heard of this, they set out to take charge of Him; for people were saying that He was out of His mind.' But (v.31) when His mother and His brothers arrived, they were certainly not able to take charge of Him. This incident, which has been carefully edited out by Matthew and Luke, clearly confirms that Mary still has no idea that Jesus was destined for a special mission, though she did later on leave Nazareth and join the women who were with Jesus and ministered to Him.

A Brief Visit to Jerusalem

After the marriage in Cana comes a visit to Jerusalem which is not recorded by the synoptics, most probably because it had no bearing on the subsequent story. Again the narrative includes what St John sees as a series of signs where the actual event may have been that Jesus wished to see if He could recruit any followers from the city. Thus an account of the cleansing of the Temple is inserted here to show the powerful effect which the ministry of Jesus would have. The interview with Nicodemus, who probably knew Jesus quite well, might have been a part of the recruiting attempt. However, it was not to be so, and the comment in 2:24–25 would seem to bear this out: 'Jesus ... would not trust himself to them ... for he could tell what was in a man'.

Jesus then left Jerusalem and travelled northwards through Judea to the Jordan valley (3:22), where his followers engaged in baptising, though there is no mention of preaching or teaching, even to them. Meanwhile, the Baptist is also there and this gives the opportunity for his further testimony that he is only the forerunner who must grow less as Jesus grows greater. It might well have been on this occasion that Jesus actually received baptism from John and that essential confirmation of the full presence of the Holy Spirit dwelling in him. After a while Jesus begins a return to Galilee through Samaria, and this journey gives rise to what must have been an actual event, but one which the apostle uses to good effect as a teaching medium (4:1–42). This is the story of Jesus and the woman at Jacob's well, the details of which St John must have obtained from her and her neighbours in Sychar. Thereafter Jesus arrives back in Galilee and the accounts begin of the start of the ministry as we read of them in the synoptics.

Chapter Seven

Conclusion

A Summary of the Arguments

In order to consider the effect of the present examination, it may be helpful to set out a summary in a series of brief statements.

1. Jesus was the natural first child of Joseph and Mary of Nazareth, clearly exceptionally gifted and of an outstanding charisma, but not otherwise different from their other four sons and at least two daughters. Joseph, a skilled craftsman, was able to provide a comfortable home and the children would have enjoyed a happy family life.

2. The doctrine of the Virgin Birth as proclaimed in the Nicene Creed is founded on later additions to the Gospels, most probably in the third century, and cannot be deduced from the Gospels.

3. The family regularly visited Jerusalem each year, would have had friends in the City, and Jesus had many opportunities to become familiar with the religious culture there and to get to know many of the leading men, both religious and lay, while still living with His family in Nazareth.

4. A carpenter at this time, and particularly one who had

close contacts with Jerusalem, would have had a wide range of tools available to him and therefore be able to exercise a high degree of skill. He would also have been a builder, perhaps what would now be called a developer, as well as a maker of all kinds of wooden artefacts for the home, the farmer and the merchant. There is thus every reason to suppose that Joseph and his family would, when his five sons were working with him, have enjoyed a fair degree of prosperity.

5. Galilee at this time was enjoying the comparatively peaceful reign of Herod Antipas. It was a fertile and well populated region with a substantial Jewish presence which would have been able to support and encourage the development of such a business.

6. The family would have been well known in Nazareth and the surrounding area and especially so in the synagogue, where Jesus had become acknowledged as a Rabbi in spite of His youth.

7. With the death of Joseph, Jesus would have become the head of the family and the carpentry business. The consequent increase in pressure on Jesus made it necessary for Him to break away from Nazareth in spite of all the difficulties this entailed, nor can the huge disappointment there be wondered at.

8. Jesus establishes a home in Capernaum where He is able to place Himself fully under the influence of the Holy Spirit and prepare for the ministry which He now knows is His true work. His stay there included the visits to Cana and to Jerusalem as recorded in St John's gospel.

9. The preaching of John the Baptist, and perhaps the discussions which Jesus had with him, persuades Him that His time has come. The baptism which He receives is the occasion for the sign that the Holy Spirit has come fully upon Him and that He is able to be obedient to the Will of His Heavenly Father.

The Divinity of Jesus

I have set out the arguments which can be summarised in the above statements, but what effect should they have on the church at large? It is said that in the minds of many people Jesus is the pale man of Nazareth, indeed He is sometimes referred to as 'the pale Galilean', whereas it must be the case that He experienced a rich and varied life there, much of which can be seen to be reflected in His parables. There should therefore stand before us on the threshold of His ministry a young Man of tremendous charisma, an acknowledged leader in Nazareth, with a reputation for a challenging erudition among the religious establishment in Jerusalem and probably already not unknown in Capernaum itself. All this had not derived from any suggestion that He had experienced a virgin birth in the manner claimed for the Caesars, or that He had come down from Heaven or enjoyed any of the titles that Christians like to claim for Him before He even began His ministry. All that it is necessary to say about Him at this time is that He was fully human and had experienced human birth as proclaimed by Wordsworth:

> ... trailing clouds of glory do we come
> From God who is our home:
> Heaven lies about us in our infancy!

How then was the divinity of Jesus attained? The apostle John, in his gospel, says that Nathanael recognised Jesus on first meeting Him and on the threshold of His ministry. 'Rabbi', he said, 'you are the Son of God; you are the king of Israel'. That must have been St John's own view, stated at the outset of his Gospel so that there could be no doubt as to the message it was to convey. For St Mark and the synoptics it was not until halfway through the ministry, when on the way to Caesarea Philippi Jesus then asked His disciples, 'Who do you say I am?', and Peter made his famous declaration: 'You are the Messiah'. Even this may only have meant to the disciples that they saw Jesus as the anointed one, chosen by God to bring back the kingdom of Israel. According to Mark, even James and John could have seen no further than this in making their request to Jesus on the road going up to Jerusalem for the last time. 'Master,' they said, 'grant us the right to sit in state with you', and were roundly told that they did not understand what they were asking.

Whatever may have been the doubts and misunderstandings of His disciples, Jesus was Himself aware of a special relationship with God the Father, signified to Him at His baptism and confirmed at His transfiguration: 'This is my Son, my Beloved'. He would have told Peter, James and John of this, as well as of that most intimate account of His temptations after baptism, but the full meaning of all this escaped them, as was only to be expected, until after His resurrection. Then at last Thomas would say for them all, 'My Lord and my God!'

What it took the disciples so long to understand was known to Jesus from the decisive moment of the baptism, was manifested in the faithful performance of the ministry, and was crowned in the ultimate obedience of the cross. By the mighty act of the resurrection and ascension, and the gift to men of the Holy Spirit, God made known to us that divinity of Jesus which the Gospels proclaim and in which the Church believes. But Jesus could not be God incarnate, though He could and did show us what God is like. He has showed us too how we may become the children of God by following His example, not least in the commitment to His family and community in Nazareth until He had to leave them. St John's meditations on the life of Jesus in his Gospel spell out how we may do this if we truly believe that 'Jesus is Lord,' the Way the Truth and the Life, that to see Him is to know God and that to eat His food is to save our souls. We too have access to the Holy Spirit in the same way that Jesus did, as the Church has always known. The Bishop prays that each confirmation candidate may be confirmed with the Holy Spirit, and with the congregation that all candidates may daily increase in the same 'more and more', in the way that Jesus Himself 'grew in favour with God'. So in the well-known hymn we sing:

> Come down, O Love Divine
> Seek Thou this soul of mine...
> For none can guess its grace
> Till he become the place
> Wherein the Holy Spirit makes its dwelling

For us to grow in grace in this way is to follow the example of Jesus in His life in Nazareth, guided by His teaching and further example in His ministry. The former is a way that we can all understand. We know what family life is like, its joys and its sorrows, its smiles and tears that Jesus shares with each of us. He was a child among several and the eldest of many, having to apply Himself to learning just as we do in the midst of the family. He faced the problems we face and can hear our prayers right from the beginning of our lives. Then, too, He was an apprentice or trainee who had to acquire a difficult craft and learn to use many tools. The special needs of customers had to be met, work had naturally to be done to the highest standards and the agreed price adhered to. We have all to go through the same process in whatever career we take up and can share our inevitable frustrations with Him. When we are equipped to launch out into the world, He has been there before us and knows the pitfalls and mistakes that can be made and is there to help us. By remembering this background when we read the Gospels, we can find how much Jesus does draw upon it and so gain new inspiration from His teaching.

The Worship of the Church
Although Jesus would have been a manager in the family

business, His preeminence must have been amongst the religious community, the congregation of the synagogue in Nazareth and His standing among the hierarchy in Jerusalem, which would have been well known to them. Throughout the Gospel accounts He is referred to as Master, Rabbi or Teacher and this popular acclaim must have had its origin in Nazareth and been confirmed in Capernaum even before He began the ministry. So His challenge to the hierarchy came from a thorough knowledge of His co-religionists, which makes His basic charge of hypocrisy all the more biting. This is a fallibility that we are all heir to and we have to remember that a similar charge can often be made against ourselves.

One area in particular where this message must not be obscured is in our forms of worship. It has been shown with a reasonable degree of certainty that Jesus was not born in any peculiar way and for that reason alone we have to abandon the Nicene Creed. This should be done in the same way that the Church of England has abandoned the Thirty Nine Articles and the Athanasian Creed, by no longer using them. The latter was formulated to correct the heretical nature of the Nicene Creed in that it contains no assertion that Jesus was Perfect Man. It concentrates far too much on statements about Jesus which are contrary to His own teaching about Himself and which cannot be infallibly proved from the Gospels. It is too long and becoming increasingly unacceptable, especially among young people. The use of the Apostles' Creed in place of it, omitting the words 'conceived by the Holy Ghost', would probably be welcomed by most Christians, since it is still in general use and much loved. It is a Creed which accords well with the *Gloria in Excelsis* in the Communion Service.

In the teaching and preaching of the Church, a greater emphasis is needed on such passages as the Sermon on the Mount and on the parables, remembering that the saving power of Jesus affects every moment of our daily lives and that He knows precisely what our problems are. He knows what family life is like, He knows what church life is like, He knows what problems our business and our work can create for us. He altogether knows the frailty of our human condition and will hear us when we bring these things to Him. It may also be very valuable for us to realise the importance of the period of preparation which Jesus experienced as a model for our own lives and our own work in the Church.

Part 2

JESUS IN TEMPTATION

Some Mysteries Explained

Introduction

In Part One I have presented what I think is a convincing case for regarding Jesus as the natural son of Joseph and Mary. To regard Him so does not in any way diminish His status as the second Person of the Holy Trinity, since that is not dependent upon the nature of His birth. That arose from the way in which His adult life was guided by the Holy Spirit, from His submission at all times to the Will of God, our heavenly Father, and of course from the mighty act of God which raised Him from the dead. What then would be the significance of a natural birth? The Church has endeavoured to teach that Jesus is both perfect Man and perfect God, which can only be regarded as an impossible concept for ordinary human beings. It is, however, a very simple concept to believe that Jesus was born in the natural way so as to become perfect Man and that His divinity as perfect God arose in the manner described above. There is ample testimony to all the attributes of His divinity, as to how and when and where, but only the place of His birth is known for certain.

A belief in His natural birth makes a very considerable

difference to our understanding of Jesus. Part One shows how it affects the gospel accounts of His youth and later the preparation for His ministry. It suggests how it can illuminate the kind of life He would have had with His family in Nazareth, in the course of His work and in His place in the synagogue. There is, however, the wider field of His public ministry which can also be illuminated in this way, including how human temptation could have guided His thoughts and actions. The Church has been accustomed to pay little heed to the temptations of Jesus as described in Matthew and Luke. The belief that as perfect God He was without sin leads to the notion that temptations could not trouble Him. Thus insufficient attention has been given to them, creating a gap in our understanding of Jesus. It is the purpose of this Part to show that there is much to learn from the very real temptations Jesus had to face and overcome. In addition, a clearer light can be shed on the true humanity of this unique Man.

Chapter 8

Human Temptation

Was Jesus Tempted?

As it is the ordinary lot of all mankind to have to face temptation, the fact that Jesus did so might well be used as a further argument in support of His natural birth. It would of course first have to be established that Jesus did experience temptations and that those He faced were real. Most commentators agree that the accounts in the Gospels of Matthew and Luke of the temptations of Jesus must have come from Him. This arises from the intrinsic link that exists between these two Gospels and that of St Mark, on which is based the belief now held by, I think, a majority of New Testament scholars that Mark's Gospel was the first to have been written and circulated in the Early Church. It is widely thought that the Gospels attributed to Matthew and Luke, having been composed subsequently to that of Mark, were able to use what he had written, though with their particular editorial adjustments of his text. Subject to this, and in general terms, almost the whole of Mark is found in the other two with the material largely used in the same order. An examination of the effect of this is given in the next chapter.

Jesus of Nazareth: A New Look

A careful study of the text of Matthew and Luke also shows that they share further material largely composed of sayings of Jesus. As a result, it is now widely accepted that some of the sayings of Jesus had already been preserved in written form and circulated in a document now lost, but which is identified as 'Q', from the German word 'Quelle' meaning source (see Part Four). 'Q' is regarded as the earliest Christian record, predating Mark and therefore equally available to the writers of Matthew and Luke. Thus it is not surprising to find that Mark records that after the baptism of Jesus 'the Spirit sent him away into the wilderness, and there He remained for forty days tempted by Satan.' No account of the temptations is given, though the details of these must have been known to St Peter, who is generally regarded as St Mark's principal informant. As 'Q' must have been known to Mark, he presumably thought it unnecessary to include these sayings in his Gospel. It might even have been the case that the consequent brevity of the latter facilitated its copying and distribution.

By the time that the Gospels of Matthew and Luke came to be written, the advantage of having the texts of Mark and 'Q' in one document was recognised, though it seems clear that each was produced independently. There is also to be found in them additional material peculiar to each. There are some variations in the two accounts of the sayings taken from 'Q', which most importantly do include the temptations, but the accounts of the latter are the same in all essentials and, because of their origin in 'Q', must be regarded as coming from Jesus himself. It seems clear that He was no stranger to temptation, for Luke records His saying to the disciples (22:28) 'You are the men who have stood firmly by me in my times of trial'. So there is this further argument in favour of regarding Jesus as the natural Son of Joseph and Mary.

Before considering the temptations in detail, it is worth while to reflect upon some further reasons for doing so. In the light of the duration of His ministry, and the amount of speaking and preaching that Jesus must have done, the extent of His sayings available to us is very small; therefore the inclusion in them of these particular trials must be significant. This is particularly so if the discourses of Jesus in St John's gospel are regarded as mainly free compositions of the Evangelist, not the *ipsissima verba*, the actual words of Jesus, as some scholars now think. The saying noted above would indicate that Jesus did face temptations during His public ministry, particularly perhaps as the growing enmity of the Jewish religious establishment began to threaten His very life. The temptation then would be to moderate His strictures upon them, but, if anything, Jesus intensifies His attacks and especially during the final period in Jerusalem. Thus the temptations at the beginning of the ministry must have been real or they would hardly have found a place in the sayings. Yet very little study or thought seems to have been given to them though they deserve it as much as any of the sayings of Jesus.

Temptations in the Family

If it is natural for us to face temptation it is also not unnatural that from time to time we give way. The extent of our failure can in the worst case lead to mortal sin, but happily for most of us our sins are not of this nature, but are venial and can be forgiven. The Christian churches have always held that Jesus was without sin, but it must have been possible for him to give way to temptation, for otherwise any that He suffered would have been no trial to Him at all. There are signs of this in connection with His dealings with His family. For most people it is probably the case that relations to and with other members of their family give rise to more sin than any other connection. This is so at any rate if sin is regarded as a falling short of standards of behaviour which we would normally expect to maintain. Our sin may be thoughtlessness, or by being provoked as we might think, or by the family's resistance to what we may wish to do. Outside the family, where we might feel greater restraints and a need to be on our best behaviour, these problems may not arise or we are more careful in our response to them.

Thus, when Jesus was a boy on that well-known visit to Jerusalem, He separated Himself from His parents and family in order to spend His time with the doctors of the law in the Temple. Unfortunately He did not let His parents know where He was to be found, so that, having begun their homeward journey, they were compelled in much anxiety to turn back to seek for Him. This no doubt was mere thoughtlessness on the part of a boy, but it would seem to show that Jesus was not without the natural human tendency to err.

Another indication of the trials that can beset even such a person as Jesus arose at the point when He had to take leave of His family and friends in Nazareth. I have already examined in some detail the position which Jesus must have come to occupy in His family, in the general community and most of all in the life of the synagogue. In each of these areas He would surely have been an outstanding figure whose decision, perhaps quite sudden, to leave Nazareth would have been a great shock to all who knew Him. Jesus may well have come to realise that His involvement in so many aspects of life in Nazareth was becoming an obstacle in the way of His true mission rather than a period of preparation for it. But by then there would be no way in which He could withdraw without some upset to His family and friends, however much He would have regretted that. It would moreover have been extremely difficult, perhaps impossible, to explain what it was He intended to do.

Trouble with His Mother and Brothers
It is not therefore altogether surprising that when His mother and brothers discovered that Jesus was setting Himself up as an itinerant preacher and appointing disciples, 'they set out to take charge of him; for people were saying that he was out of his mind' (Mark 3:21). When they eventually found Him,

Jesus in Temptation

Jesus had entered a house and was talking to His disciples and some doctors of the law who had come down from Jerusalem. 'Then his mother and his brothers arrived and, remaining outside, sent in a message asking him to come out to them ... word was brought to him ... He replied: Who is my mother? Who are my brothers?' (Mark 3:31–33). Jesus went on to say that, 'Whoever does the will of God is my brother, my sister, my mother,' but there is no record that He met His mother and brothers and, if this was indeed the case, they must have returned to Nazareth quite hurt and perplexed, unable to understand that Jesus was now about His Father's business. It would have been so completely out of character for Jesus not to have met them that I feel sure that He did, and persuaded them to have confidence in him.

Chapter 9

The True Jesus Only Found in St Mark's Gospel

St Mark's account of the visit of His family undoubtedly caused a difficulty in the Early Church as it seemed to show Jesus in an unfavourable light and in an unforgiving mood towards them. Thus neither Matthew nor Luke records the reason given by Mark noted above (3:21) for the visit of His mother and brothers. They do, however, record the visit itself and the comment which it drew from Jesus. He Himself no doubt understood the position as it is explained by Mark and did not wish to become embroiled in what might have become an unseemly family dispute. But the omission of this reason by the other two synoptics makes the situation worse, allowing Jesus to reject His family for no apparent cause. On this score, therefore, it may well be argued that they confirm the story as given by Mark. So it sometimes is that what may begin as an understandable difference within a family can be made more difficult when friends and well-wishers intervene without a full knowledge of what has occurred.

A Visit to Nazareth

The failure of His family and His friends properly to understand what Jesus was doing seems to be reflected in their
behaviour towards Him when, in the course of the public
ministry, He visited Nazareth with His disciples (Mark 6:1),
perhaps in the hope of being reconciled to them. We do not
know whether He stayed with His family, only that at first
He is accorded His apparently usual status in the synagogue,
where he is expected to choose the reading and to preach
from it. What He had to say to the large congregation,
however, clearly aroused their disappointment, not to say
anger, 'so they fell foul of him' (Mark 6:4), but neither Mark
nor Matthew, who closely follows the former's account, give
any indication of what it was that Jesus said on that occasion.

The account of this visit in Luke's Gospel, however, identifies the passage which Jesus read and the principal points
He made in His address (4:18–27), information which could
have been obtained from the mother of Jesus or from the
disciples who had accompanied Him. The account states that
some members of the congregation were ready even to take
His life or at least to place Him in danger. They might
perhaps have claimed that Jesus provoked them by His
explanation of why He did not repeat in His home town, the
miracles of healing which it was widely known had been
done in Capernaum. Jesus remarked that He might be without honour in his own country, but likened His situation to
that of Elijah and Elisha. The former, when there was famine
in Israel, 'was sent to a widow in Sidon', while the latter,
when there were many lepers in Israel, healed only Naaman
the Syrian. This account, like that of the boy Jesus in the
Temple in Jerusalem, must have been obtained by Luke from
His mother. It is not unreasonable to wonder whether the
degree of worldly success which Jesus had previously attained
in Nazareth had become something of a temptation which
made it difficult to bring about a harmonious departure from

53

His family and friends and made this visit a cause of friction. However, we know that later on His mother was among the women who accompanied Him, was indeed present at His crucifixion, and that His brothers were with His disciples thereafter. There must have been forgiveness on both sides, though at the time of His visit to Nazareth the message Jesus wished to convey must have been misunderstood.

The Differences in the Gospels

The incidents reviewed above show that Jesus might have behaved in a similar way to any normal member of a family or community. This is more especially so in the accounts given by St Mark and there are events in the public ministry that bear this out. On several occasions Jesus disputed with the Pharisees over their rules for the observance of the Sabbath. Once, in the synagogue, 'they were watching to see whether Jesus would cure a man who had a withered arm on the Sabbath'. He asked them whether it was permitted to do so and they had nothing to say. 'Looking round at them with anger and sorrow at their obstinate stupidity', Jesus healed the man and they thereupon began plotting 'to see how they could make away with him' (Mark 3:1–6). Matthew and Luke give a similar account, but omit the reference to the anger and sorrow shown by Jesus as if it were unfitting for the Son of God to show such righteous indignation. This omission, as with that of the reason for the visit of His mother and brothers, gravely weakens the character of Jesus as presented in these two Gospels and might throw doubt on the veracity of Mark. In such cases, however, it is sounder to accept the version that appears to be critical, particularly bearing in mind that it most probably came from the lips of St Peter. The alterations, mainly omissions, which Matthew and Luke make when using the text of Mark's Gospel, reflect the increasing tendency of the Early Church, and the predilection of the modern Church, to obscure the humanity of Jesus and to regard Him as the risen and ascended Lord from the very beginning of His ministry. There can be no doubt that His unique obedience to the Will of Our Father in Heaven, to use his own terminology, brought Him in the end to that divine status. Nevertheless it is perfectly possible for the power of the Holy Spirit to have grown in Him through the periods of preparation in Nazareth and Capernaum, marked the beginning of His ministry at His Baptism and revealed something of His final nature at the Transfiguration. Such a progression would allow full account to be taken of other descriptions of the humanity of Jesus found in Mark which have been changed by Matthew and Luke, but which are very relevant to a study of His temptations. Thus, when to test Him the Pharisees asked for a sign from heaven, 'He sighed deeply to himself' (Mark 8:12) and this is not included by the other two. On being asked by a leper for His help, Mark records that 'in warm indignation ... Jesus touched him' (1:41) and, again, when the disciples scolded people for bringing children to him, Jesus 'was indignant' and 'blessed them lovingly' (Mark 10:14,15), but both His indignation and His love are omitted by the other two. So when Jesus met the man who wanted to know how to win eternal life, 'His heart warmed to him' (Mark 10:21), but this too is omitted.

Jesus and Simon Peter
By these omissions Jesus is made to appear as a quite colourless individual, the pale man of Galilee as He is sometimes called, but which He most certainly was not. One other example of this kind of editing was no doubt intended to protect the reputation of St Peter as much as to soften the vehemence of Jesus, even though Mark's account was given to him by Peter. At a point at least halfway through the ministry He had set out with the disciples for the villages of Caesarea Philippi, and on the way He asked them, 'Who do you say I am?' Peter had made his famous declaration, 'You are the Messiah' (Mark 8:30). Then, according to the account in Matthew (16:17–20), Jesus had singularly praised Peter,

had bestowed upon him the title 'the Rock' and declared that upon that rock the Church would be built and that Peter would be given great authority. In both accounts Jesus had then warned the disciples that He would have to undergo great sufferings and to be put to death. 'He spoke about it plainly. At this Peter took him by the arm and began to rebuke him. But Jesus turned round, and, looking at his disciples, rebuked Peter, "Away with you, Satan," he said; "you think as men think, not as God thinks"' (Mark 8:33). Luke omits this exchange of rebukes entirely and, while Matthew includes it, he first inserts that long paean of praise of Peter from the lips of Jesus that would certainly not have been found in 'Q', and sits rather oddly in the narrative. While there is no doubt that Peter earned his supremacy in the Early Church it is most unlikely that Jesus would have addressed him so at this stage and then immediately after-wards have called him Satan. Mark's unadorned account must then stand and clearly reveals a man to man relation-ship between Jesus and His disciples.

Jesus and His Disciples

St Mark does in fact make it very clear that Jesus placed Himself alongside the disciples in his attitude towards God, the Father of all mankind. This is particularly so in the following anecdote: 'a stranger ran up and, kneeling before him, asked, "Good Master, what must I do to win eternal life?" Jesus said to him "Why do you call me good? No one is good except God alone"' (Mark 10:17,18). St Luke repeats this exactly, but Matthew makes some changes, having the man say, 'Master, what good must I do to gain eternal life?' 'Good?' said Jesus. 'Why do you ask me about that? One alone is good.' The tenor of these accounts is perfectly clear. Jesus did not identify Himself with God, though He did not conceal His unique intimate closeness to His and our Heavenly Father, which separates Him from the rest of mankind.

This analysis of the way in which Jesus is presented in the

Jesus in Temptation

gospel according to St Mark gives further evidence of His real humanity and so emphasises the need to take seriously the temptations which He faced. We can then give heartfelt agreement to the words of the collect that is set for 25th April, when St Mark the Evangelist is commemorated:

'Almighty God, you have enlightened your holy Church through the inspired witness of your evangelist Saint Mark. Grant that we, being firmly grounded in the truth of the gospel, may be faithful to its teaching...'

Chapter 10

The Reality of the Temptations of Jesus

The Garden of Gethsemane
(See also Chapter 14)

The events in the public ministry indicated above show what enormous pressures Jesus had to overcome and make clear that His reactions are very much of the same order as our own. Jesus had by this time been given clear indications of the fate that would await Him if He were to continue on the course He had chosen to follow, though His disciples seemed to be completely unaware of the danger their Master was facing. A final and perhaps the most complete example of the temptations which Jesus suffered, and the inability of his friends to understand the situation, occurred in the garden of Gethsemane to which He went with His disciples after the Last Supper. A full account of this will be found in Chapter 14. It is not possible to contemplate the scene there without receiving a profound sense that it fully reveals the humanity of Jesus. He had already followed a course of action which He believed to be in accordance with the Will of His heavenly Father by allowing Judas to betray Him. He could easily have gone elsewhere than to Gethsemane and so defeated the misguided disciple, whose intention was, it seems, to force Jesus to declare Himself as a political leader of the Jews. He must have known, however, that if He avoided this trap another would be set for Him, for His enemies were by now implacable. Nevertheless, the realisation of the sufferings and cruel torture which death by crucifixion would bring upon Him must have been terrible indeed. Having arrived at the fateful place, the temptation even yet to escape from what lay ahead is only too clearly revealed in the anguished words of Jesus. We note also His acute awareness of the contrast between His own situation and the sleepful ease of His friends. This is no make-believe of a divine persona playing a part, but the horror of a man whose 'heart is ready to break with grief' (Mark 14:34). This surely is because at this point Jesus not only foresees His own death, but also the collapse of His mission, the scattering of His followers and total failure. Yet further prayer convinces Him that He must continue to trust in His heavenly Father, a spirit of calm possesses Him and He boldly faces the crowd armed with swords and cudgels who come to arrest Him.

The various temptations and trials that Jesus experienced as described above make it clear that in this respect He shared our common humanity. They were real to Him, as is most convincingly illustrated by what took place in the Garden of Gethsemane. Thus it is not unreasonable to attribute to a boy's thoughtlessness the worry caused to His parents when He became lost to them in Jerusalem. We may understand, too, the difficulties which He experienced with His family at the outset of His ministry. It is important that we should recognise that this is so in order to give a proper weight to the temptations which Jesus experienced even before He began the ministry. It is now expedient to examine the accounts of them which we have in the Gospels of Matthew and Luke.

Jesus Describes his Temptations

As noted above, it is generally accepted that these two Gospels are based on that of St Mark. There are in Matthew and Luke words attributed to Jesus which have clearly come from the same source and are often identical. These, it is believed, must have been taken from 'Q', and the accounts of the temptations must surely come into this category. It could be objected, of course, that these accounts are not sayings of Jesus, but it is not conceivable that there could be any other origin for them other than the document 'Q'. If they were an invention it is improbable that Matthew, whose gospel was almost certainly written in Antioch, would have the same version as Luke, who was most probably writing in Corinth. The accounts are so strikingly similar that they *must* have come from the same source, namely 'Q', and must therefore be attributed to Jesus Himself. Equally, if they cannot be regarded as invention there could be no other source for them but Jesus and for this reason they deserve careful study, for they must have deeply influenced the course which Jesus was to follow in His public ministry. Our purpose, therefore, is to give them that careful examination which all the undoubted sayings of Jesus ought to receive.

At this point we should pause to reflect upon the Man whose trials we are to consider. Luke tells us that He was about 30 years old (3:23) at the time of His baptism. He would have been mature and experienced in the ways of the world as a result of His upbringing in Nazareth and confident that He had set out upon the path which His heavenly Father had made clear to Him. There rang in His ears the words He had heard as He emerged from the water: 'Thou art my Son, my Beloved; on thee my favour rests (Mark 1:11). He had probably spent some 18 months in Capernaum in retreat from His worldly success in Nazareth, a time of prayer and contemplation as well as an opportunity to meet some of the men who were to become His disciples. He had been able to form a plan of campaign, as we would say, though there were clearly problems as to how the spiritual powers with which He now felt endowed should be used. So Jesus withdraws into the complete solitude of the wild and desertlike country beyond the Jordan in order to think more deeply about this aspect of His mission. He explains the difficulties He foresaw in the form of three separate temptations.

Chapter 11

The First Temptation

Its Description

There is no difficulty in identifying this because both Luke and Matthew place it first in their accounts and it must have been so placed in 'Q'. They vary as to the order of the other two, which might be due to the editorial choice of one of them or to the copies of that lost document not being in agreement because of some error in transcription. It is, however, of little consequence since the Evangelists agree as to the nature of the temptations. We can, therefore, follow the most usual order as set by Matthew in the opening verses of Chapter 4 – usual, no doubt, because his gospel has been placed first.

In the wilderness Jesus would certainly have been hungry, living perhaps as the Baptist had done on locusts and wild honey. So it was that the tempter said to Him, 'If you are the Son of God, tell these stones to become bread.' The reply He made was to quote the Mosaic Law: 'Man cannot live on bread alone; he lives on every word that God utters'. The temptation was not surely the immediate satisfaction of bodily hunger by an interference with the laws of nature, but the way in which the spiritual power which Jesus felt He would now be able to exercise should be used. The Jews believed that the coming of the Messiah would herald an age of material prosperity, and Jesus had to consider to what extent, if at all, He would address that particular aspiration. It was not in itself a thing to be avoided, yet it could become all consuming, as Jesus had no doubt discovered as a result of His successful business career in Nazareth.

Feeding the Multitude
In the course of His ministry, Jesus was frequently in the presence of large crowds which speedily assembled as soon as He was known to have arrived in a place. This was even the case when He was found in a lonely place where He had wished to retire with His disciples. In two such instances, as recorded by Mark (6:30 and 8:1), the question soon arose as to how all these people could be fed. The disciples were for turning them away, but Jesus had a better idea. According to the Evangelist, in each case He took a few loaves and fishes and distributed them so that all were fed and there was much left over. Many would regard this as a poetical way of explaining what they think took place, for a literal miracle would have been a submission to the temptation we have been considering.

It can reasonably be assumed that the people involved had come from the towns and villages round about and that most of them would have brought some food with them, but they probably would be strangers to each other. Mark indeed records that Jesus thought they were like sheep without a shepherd, lacking any unifying force. It would therefore be something of a miracle if they could be persuaded to pool whatever food was available and share it out. Jesus was obviously the person who could make them do this and Mark's repetition of the story in a slightly different form might well indicate that it happened on several occasions. It was surely a splendid illustration of one of the ways in which we have to learn to live together and share out the bountiful riches of the natural world, and there is still so much need for us to follow this teaching. By regarding what took place as a miracle, the work of Jesus alone, we may not learn anything from it at all and would have to admit that He succumbed to the temptation to interfere with the laws of nature.

On the other hand, as all the Evangelists present this story as the work of Jesus, they were almost certainly using it to show the importance of the Eucharistic Meal for the members of the newly formed Christian churches. That lesson has been learned and in the Anglican Church has been consolidated by a positive move, replacing the Sunday morning service of Matins by that of the Parish Communion. So now it may be better to adopt a simple and quite natural interpretation of what took place and to take very much to heart the lesson that flows from it. We shall be much nearer to the Kingdom of Heaven when we have learned throughout the world to share with one another the fruits of the harvest.

In a similar way, St John has taken his version of the feeding of the multitude (John 6:1–13) as a sign that Jesus will be the bread of life to all that believe in Him. He makes it a deliberate act of Jesus on the hillside above the Sea of Galilee, not as a consequence of preaching in a desert place. There was no apparent need for the people to be fed in a material sense, but St John finds the occasion of the feeding to have great significance in the teaching and remembering of the gospel.

Water into Wine?

There is a similar situation with the turning of water into wine at the wedding in Cana (John 2:1–11). It is not conceivable that Jesus would have wanted to create so large a supply of new wine just as the wedding feast must have been drawing to a close. The wine the guests had consumed would by modern standards have been thought a pretty rough vintage. The cool water of purification was not normally used for drinking but, Jesus as a local Rabbi having sanctioned its use, the wedding guests would have found it most refreshing to the palate. It may well have been this circumstance that inspired St John to use the event as a sign of what the coming of Jesus would achieve. The new wine of the gospel would be immeasurably superior to the rough wine delivered in the teaching of the Pharisees and the doctors of the law who comprised the Jewish establishment. This explanation may be one which is becoming generally more acceptable to the Church. It would, moreover, surely have been the case that if a miracle of such a kind had been performed by Jesus it would have been mentioned in one of the other gospels.

Chapter 12

The Second Temptation

Its Description

Following the order used by St Matthew, we read:

The devil then took him to the Holy City and set him on the parapet of the temple. 'If you are the Son of God,' he said, 'throw yourself down; for Scripture says, "He will put his angels in charge of you, and they will support you in their arms, for fear you should strike your foot against a stone."' Jesus answered him, 'Scripture says again, "You are not to put the Lord your God to the test."'

If that had really been a temptation to which Jesus might have succumbed, what a spectacle it would have made! Demonstrations of this kind cannot, however, have been occupying the mind of Jesus. There would be much subtler ways in which the power He now knew Himself to possess could be exercised, but which would not be in accordance with the Will of His heavenly Father. Our purpose therefore is to consider what those ways may have been and whether there are any signs of them in the gospel stories as we have them. So far as the former is concerned, any action that interfered with the laws of nature would seem to be involved. Many of the miracles of healing which are attributed to Jesus in all the gospels might be regarded as coming under this head. It must have been the case, however, that the impact of the personal power, the magnetism and the general charisma of Jesus on those who came into contact with Him must have been immense. Moreover, His understanding of people was so profound that it is easy to see how His dealings with them must have seemed quite miraculous. We cannot therefore regard the accounts of the miracles of healing as being involved in this study. It would only be where people are not directly involved, and the attribution of a miracle would appear to be unnecessary, that the story should be more closely examined. There are in fact very few such incidents, but they have a considerable importance in the tradition of the church and are deserving of study.

Quelling the Storm?

The first to occur in the gospel narratives is the story of a sudden storm on the Sea of Galilee and before considering it we have to set the scene. This small inland sea or Lake of Tiberias is known to be subject to squalls which are more alarming for their suddenness of coming and going than for their actual danger. The fishermen among the disciples of Jesus would be well accustomed to the peculiarities of their watery environment and competent to deal with them. The fishing boats which they used were almost certainly undecked, except perhaps for a small locker in the bow for storage of gear; the decking over this might have had a low spray shield. The means of propulsion would be oars which could be shipped to give maximum clearance when handling nets. The crew would probably number no more than four, though two might manage if they were not fishing. The disciples who were not fishermen would not have been at ease aboard such a craft and may not have been aware that sudden squalls might be met.

We can now consider the story in its fullest version as told by St Mark (4:35–41), though most of it is repeated in both Matthew and Luke. It is evening and Jesus suggests to His disciples that they should cross to the other side of the lake, so they set out in the boat in which He had been sitting. There were other boats with them, though it is most interesting to note that neither Matthew nor Luke mentions the other boats. It would be unlikely that all the disciples could have crowded into the same boat, but three or four might have joined Jesus and perhaps two of the four fishermen, Andrew, Peter, James and John. The other disciples must have been in the accompanying boats and their presence would have been a reassuring feature. Jesus, who was no doubt accustomed to going out with the fishermen, was asleep on a cushion in the stern when a heavy squall came on and the waves began to break over the boat. It was now essential that the passengers should keep still, out of the way of the oarsmen, lying down if possible, but it seems they would not do this and began to panic, ignoring the shouts of the fishermen. So they aroused Jesus who, when He woke up, immediately grasped the situation and said, 'Hush! Be still! Why are you such cowards? Have you no faith even now?'

It would seem most likely that Jesus was addressing the frightened disciples, but as the squall blew over as suddenly as it had come, they may well have told the story as though the words 'Hush! Be still!' had been a command to the storm. This is the way it has been told by the Evangelists, with Matthew making Jesus stand up and rebuke the wind and the sea. The danger in the situation, however, was not the storm but the presence of passengers, who had not been told what to do in such an emergency. That Jesus was still sleeping should have made them realise that the oarsmen knew what to do and to have faith in them as well as in Him. That such a miracle was attributed to Jesus is not surprising, given the circumstances, but it is unlikely that there was real danger and such an interference with the laws of nature was precisely what Jesus had determined would not be His way. Better by far that we should always be aware of natural hazards, take sensible precautions and have faith in our fellow Christians. Nevertheless, the version of the story as given by Matthew has become so firmly the tradition of the Church that Jesus is saddled with an act which is clearly not in accordance with His way.

Walking on Water?

The next incident is also concerned with the Sea of Galilee, in a story that not only has Jesus walking on the water as related by Mark (6:45–52) and John (6:16–21), but in Matthew (14:22–34) has Peter endeavouring to do so as well. Luke, however, has no record of it. The account given in John agrees very well with that in Mark, in particular placing it during the night after the feeding of the five thousand. It is not now supposed that the author of John's gospel made any use of Mark's. Moreover, the latter is thought to have been composed *circa* AD 60, while the former is not reckoned to have been produced until the end of the first century. This must indicate that the story was very popular in the Early Church as emphasising the divinity of Jesus. This is perhaps even more so in the account in Matthew which, though clearly based on Mark, places it in a quite different context in which it does not fit very well. There is then added the story of Peter's failed attempt to leave the boat and walk over the water to Jesus, who has to rescue him. Luke, although he included the stilling of the tempest, could not accept walking on the water and Matthew's addition of Peter was unknown to Mark, whose principal source was Peter and who did not conceal his mentor's weaknesses.

Since to walk on the water would have been a very gross interference with the laws of nature, and an act comparable to leaping off the pinnacle of the Temple, some explanation of the story must be sought. It seems very likely that the boat, or boats if all the disciples were involved, may well have been moving parallel with the shore, a reasonable course to follow at night when other direction finding marks might not have been visible. Against the head wind recorded by Mark and Matthew, the oarsmen would have made little progress so that Jesus, walking along the shore, may well have caught them up. The sharp eyes of the fishermen would have seen Jesus clearly enough, but the other disciples, staring through the spindrift and battered by the wind, could be excused for thinking that Jesus was walking on the water. What another splendid story that makes for them! It might indeed have been the case that Peter, intending to assist Jesus to come aboard, and thinking the water was not too deep, leapt out of the boat. Then, finding himself out of his depth, or unable to keep his footing because of the waves, he called for Jesus to help him. All the accounts agree that Jesus did come aboard and completed the journey with His friends. Some preachers may like to use this story, but I do not think there is much to be gained from it and would agree with Luke in his omission of it.

Calling down Fire?

There is one further incident worth considering which is only to be found in Luke and is at the beginning of that section of his Gospel (9:51) which covers the final journey of Jesus and His followers to Jerusalem. As they set out, He sent messengers ahead who 'went into a Samaritan village to make arrangements for him; but the villagers would not have him because he was making for Jerusalem.' At other times Jesus had been well received in Samaria and every Christian knows about the 'Good Samaritan'. When the messengers reported back, it is not surprising that the disciples displayed some anger at this rejection. Luke continues: 'When the disciples James and John saw this they said, "Lord, may we call down fire from heaven to burn them up?" But he turned and rebuked them, and they went on to another village.' The story has the brevity of the original temptations and the suggestion made meets the same response from Jesus. It is fascinating to consider how Luke could have come by it, with its deserved rebuke of two of the closest friends of Jesus. It is very likely that by this time Mary, the mother of Jesus, would have been one of the group of women who accompanied Him and she might well have been Luke's informant. The fact that it shows these two leading disciples in a bad light must be evidence of its truth and demonstrates again that Jesus had to face temptations even from those who were nearest to him. It shows, too, how difficult it was to bring them to a right understanding of His gospel of peace and goodwill. We may reflect that 2000 years of Christian teaching have not lessened the difficulty of bringing that about in our own time.

Chapter 13

The Third Temptation

Its Description

Continuing to follow the order set by St Matthew, we read (4:8):

> 'Once again, the devil took him to a very high mountain and showed him all the kingdoms of the world in their glory. "All these," he said, "I will give you, if you will only fall down and do me homage." But Jesus said, "Begone, Satan! Scripture says, "You shall do homage to the Lord your God and worship him alone'." Then the devil left him.'

At the time of Jesus, the known world comprised the Roman Empire covering the whole of the Mediterranean basin, though there were the mysterious lands of the orient, which had seen the conquests of Alexander the Great, but had not been incorporated in the empire of Rome. The kingdoms of this world might not have been visible from its highest mountain, but they were unquestionably under the gaze of the Roman Emperor. The Jews would have had no hesitation in regarding the wearer of the imperial purple as a satanic figure and Jesus would have had to take his existence into consideration as He contemplated the nature of His intended mission. This was therefore no empty temptation that He now faced. As subsequent events would show, the presence of so charismatic a person as Jesus, though on the eastern fringe of the Empire, could have had tremendous repercussions and even the bringing of that empire into the kingdom of heaven. Yet any attempt at the fusion of that kingdom with such an empire would be bound to lead to disaster and an altogether different route had to be followed. Nevertheless, there would be pitfalls on any route and some of these are clearly revealed in the gospel stories as we may now see.

Jesus not a Political Leader

The mission which Jesus was about to undertake was to free the Jewish people from the tyrannies of the detailed observance of the rules which centuries of rabbinical teaching had firmly grafted on to the simple precepts of the Mosaic law, and to introduce the more liberal concepts of the kingdom of heaven. While this proved enormously popular with the common people, it inevitably aroused the fierce resistance of the rabbinical establishment, particularly, of course, the Pharisees and the doctors of the law; the former because they were dedicated to the most exact observance of those rules and the latter because they were the teachers and upholders of them. The relations which developed on the one hand between Jesus and the ordinary Jewish people and on the other with both the latter groups had political overtones of the kind that were involved in the third temptation.

Jesus Well Known in Jerusalem *(See Part Three)*

I have suggested in Part One that, by the time Jesus began His ministry, He was already quite well known in Jerusalem, particularly to those who frequented the Temple, as a highly attractive figure and a powerful speaker. He might already have given clear indications of His desire to liberate the people from the excesses of the Pharisees and aroused some hostility among the Jewish establishment on that account. Thus, on learning that He was preaching and teaching in Galilee, they sent emissaries to keep watch upon Him. One of the ways in which their ire was specially aroused came from the views which Jesus expressed about the keeping of the Sabbath. The Law of Moses required the cessation of ordinary work, making it a day of rest, of study and of worship, but inevitably requiring a definition of work. Over the centuries quite ridiculous rules had been developed, according to which it was hardly possible to do anything. Thus Jesus and His disciples were accused of defiling the Sabbath when they plucked ears of corn when walking through a cornfield on that day, but even doing good could be wrong.

Healing on the Sabbath

The gospels record several occasions when Jesus effected a cure on the Sabbath. After one such quite early on, when a man's withered arm was healed (Mark 3:1–6), 'the Pharisees, on leaving the synagogue, began plotting against him with the partisans of Herod to see how they could make away with him.' In his version of the same incident, Luke writes that, 'they were beside themselves with anger.' Not all the Pharisees had such an enmity against Jesus, for Luke refers (13:32) to some who came to Him with a warning to leave Galilee because Herod was out to kill Him. The significant thing is that both the Jewish establishment and those who supported the Roman power, ie the partisans of Herod, were apparently joining together in their opposition to Jesus. Both regarded Him already as a threat to their control of the people and we can see at once how difficult it was going to be for Jesus to continue His ministry without some major disturbance arising. The gospels give clear indications of this, as we shall see.

Dissension as Described by St John

It is however in St John's gospel that such clashes are most vividly portrayed. The deep love and veneration which John certainly had for Jesus caused him to see the Jews in the most unfavourable light. He also had a better knowledge of the Jewish establishment than did the other Evangelists, as witness his ability to gain access to the High Priest's house after the arrest of Jesus, assuming that he was 'the other disciple, the high Priest's acquaintance' referred to in John 18:16. So we find in John's account of the feeding of the five thousand that the result of it was to make Jesus aware that the people 'meant to come and seize him to proclaim him king', so He withdrew again to the hills by Himself. (John 6:14,15) Mark says that Jesus just sent the people away, but it would not be in the least surprising if they did wish to acclaim Him as their leader. This would have had quite as much a political as a religious element, and Jesus must have been keenly aware of the danger both to Himself and his friends, as well as to the people themselves, if any such wish had been allowed to develop.

The combined effect upon the Jewish hierarchy of the preaching of Jesus and His powerful healing ministry among the Jews is shown by St John in his report of a special meeting of the chief priests and the Pharisees in their Council (John 11:47–53). 'What action are we taking?' they said. 'This man is performing many signs. If we leave him alone like this the whole populace will believe in him. Then the Romans will come and sweep away our temple and our nation.' The High Priest then advised, 'It is more to your interest that one man should die for the people than that the whole nation should be destroyed.' The story then concludes: 'So from that day on they plotted his death.' We know that this Council was not unanimous in its hostility towards Jesus, though those members who took a more favourable view of Him may not openly have declared themselves. As St John also had a link of some kind in the High Priest's house, he may well have been the recipient of what would now be called a 'leak'. There would therefore seem to be good reason to accept John's report as authentic, and it must equally be supposed that Jesus would be aware of it.

Jesus Occupies the Temple in Jerusalem

There now comes the famous entry into Jerusalem, celebrated every Palm Sunday. Jesus must have intended to attract the plaudits of the crowd, whose number would have been greatly swelled by the pilgrims arriving for the Passover festival. In this He unquestionably succeeded, and all the gospels record it. Mark tells us that they shouted, 'Hosanna! Blessings on him who comes in the name of the Lord! Blessings on the coming kingdom of our father David!' (11:8–10). The latter cry was clearly a threat to the rule of Rome, but Jesus had come in peace, riding in humility on an ass, making no threats against the civil power. Thus, on entering Jerusalem, He went straight to the Temple to show that His activity was directed there, and persuaded the people to disperse. How tempting it must have been to exploit such a success, but that had never been His way.

On the next day He returned to the Temple and implemented His opposition to what went on there by His cleansing of it. The precincts of the temple at that time comprised the great platform built by Herod the Great, most of which still exists. The southern half of this formed the court of the Gentiles and was, as its name implies, open for public access. On the east side of this court were the Porch of Solomon and the Beautiful Gate leading to the Mount of Olives, and on the west was the gate to the city. Under an arcade of Corinthian columns along the longer south side were the tables of the money changers, who were needed to enable Roman and other coins to be exchanged for the Jewish temple money which alone was acceptable for the treasury. The stalls of the sellers of small birds and the animals used for ritual sacrifices would probably have occupied most of the rest of the Court.

The northern half of the platform was at a slightly higher level, with a low wall separating it from the southern portion, and was in two parts. To the east was the Court of Women, to which no Gentiles could be admitted and where the treasury was located. This in turn gave access to the Temple podium on the western side, through a succession of open spaces, steps and balustrades. Here only males could enter, worshippers to prepare their sacrifices in the Court of Israel and the priests to have access to the Temple building where the rituals would be performed.

The sale of birds and animals, rather than worshippers bringing their own, inevitably led to a kind of market in the Court of the Gentiles, with all the noisy haggling that this would entail. In the same way, there would no doubt have been arguments about money changing, the whole scene being crowded and confused. Through the middle of it all there would have been some kind of passage way leading out of the city, regulated perhaps by the temple police. We can now appreciate the action that Jesus took, as described by St Mark:

'He went into the temple and began driving out those who bought and sold. He upset the tables of the money changers and the seats of the dealers in pigeons; and he would not allow anyone to use the temple court as a thoroughfare for carrying goods. Then he began to teach them and said, "Does not scripture say 'My house shall be called a house of prayer for all nations?' But you have made it a robbers' cave"' (11:15–18).

The triumphal entry into Jerusalem made it quite evident that Jesus was able to exercise extraordinary power over the common people. The cleansing of the Temple reveals His ability to impose His will upon the established practices at the very heart of the Jewish religion. Moreover, having purged the Temple, Jesus apparently takes it over and continues to teach there day by day throughout what we now call Holy Week. The whole Jewish establishment were, of course, infuriated beyond measure 'and sought some means of making away with him; for they were afraid of him, because the whole crowd was spellbound by his teaching' (Mark 11:18). It is not therefore surprising that St John, who liked to use significant events in the ministry of Jesus as signs of His greatness, placed his account of the cleansing at the forefront of his Gospel. Being the only one of the Evangelists to be a witness of it, he is able to add some detail. According to him, 'Jesus made a whip of cords and drove them out of the temple, sheep, cattle and all. He upset the tables of the money-changers, scattering their coins' (John 2:15). St John's intention in using the event in this way, and not in its historical position at the beginning of Holy Week, was a literary device. He desired to show that the Lordship of Jesus began from the commencement of His ministry, but in fact it would surely have been tempting fate for Jesus to have acted in this way at that time. Even so, it was only some three years later, with relatively few visits to Jerusalem during that period, and already Jesus could exercise such complete dominance in the Temple itself and such unchallengeable authority as was revealed in the next few days.

Chapter 14

In the Garden of Gethsemane

The Plan Evolved by Judas Iscariot *(See Appendix)*
It is now clear that Jesus must have been facing enormous temptations, such as face every popular leader. His own disciples must surely have been thrilled beyond measure to see the way their Master was now, as it were, at the pinnacle of the Temple, 'the crowd spellbound by his teaching' (Mark 11:19). One of them, Judas Iscariot, wanted a confrontation with the Jewish authorities, the high priests and the rulers of the Temple, which he was sure Jesus would win because the crowd would be His defence. Judas was neither able to persuade Jesus to take this course nor to understand why He would not, and evidently decided on his own way to bring it about, only to find that it led to disaster. Jesus knew of this plot and told His disciples so at the Last Supper when He said, 'I tell you this: one of you will betray me – one who is eating with me' (Mark 14:18). From the time He knew of it, Jesus must continually have been facing the temptation to avoid placing Himself in the power of men who were His implacable enemies.

In the Garden

That Jesus genuinely faced a real and terrible temptation is made abundantly clear in the account of what happened in the garden of Gethsemane, as given by St Mark, who has the fullest version. St John confirms the visit to the garden but makes no mention of what took place there. Perhaps he was ashamed at having been found asleep with the others and could not know what had transpired. What is certain is that the record we have can only have come from Jesus, for no follower or disciple of His could possibly have invented what we find in Mark. He records that Jesus spoke directly to Peter and the words must have seared into his memory: 'He took Peter and James and John with him. Horror and dismay came over him and he said to them: "My heart is ready to break with grief; stop here and stay awake." Then he went forward a little ... and prayed that, if it were possible, this hour might pass him by. "Abba, Father," he said, "...take this cup away from me."' Then there follows the most poignant of submissions: 'Yet not what I will, but what thou wilt.' 'Jesus returned and found the disciples asleep and said to Peter, "Asleep, Simon? ... Stay awake, all of you, and pray that you may be spared the test."' Twice more Jesus went away and prayed and each time He returned to find them asleep 'and they did not know how to answer him'. At the third time He said to them, 'Still sleeping? Still taking your ease? Enough! The hour has come ... My betrayer is upon us.' (Mark 14:32–42, extracts).

What Jesus knew, and His disciples could not understand, was that He faced arrest by his enemies, the certainty of a most horrible death by crucifixion, His friends deserting Him, and Simon, whom He had Himself named Peter, the Rock, denying all knowledge of Him. It was then no wonder that Jesus 'threw himself on the ground and prayed that, if it were possible, this hour might pass him by. "Abba, Father, all things are possible to thee; take this cup away from me".' No wonder that this is referred to as the agony of Jesus, for what extremes of horror must have been present in the mind of One whose understanding of the human condition could not be surpassed. How strong must have been the temptation to escape before His betrayer should come upon Him. How profound then the submission of Jesus to what He knew His heavenly Father expected of Him: 'Yet not what I will, but what thou wilt.' The conquest of that temptation has inspired Christian martyrs through the ages and ever will do so.

John Mark Keeps Awake

An extraordinary aspect of this terrible event is that when Jesus returned to His disciples He found that they had been unable to keep watch while He prayed, but were asleep. How then do we know what happened in the Garden that night, so awesome in tragedy, so divine in resolution? The only satis-factory answer must be that St Mark himself was the witness who did stay awake. He records in his gospel that when Jesus was arrested, 'Among those following was a young man with nothing on but a linen cloth. They tried to seize him, but he slipped out of the linen cloth and ran away naked' (Mark 14:51,52). It can hardly be doubted that the young man was John Mark, since only he could have been aware of such intimate details. There is little doubt that the Last Supper took place in the upper room of the house occupied by Mary, the mother of St Mark. He, therefore, awakened perhaps by hearing the disciples singing the Passover hymn before leav-ing the house, hastily flung a linen cloth around himself and followed them. He knew they had taken swords with them and very likely scented both danger and excitement. He would have kept hidden for fear of being sent home had he been discovered by the disciples and this may have enabled him to see the evident distress of Jesus and to overhear His anguished exclamations. Later on, St Peter, who is tradition-ally regarded as his principal source, would have agreed that his account did indeed disclose the agony which Jesus suffered as He wrestled with the temptation to avoid what was to come and which the disciples were neither aware of nor understood.

Chapter 15

Conclusions

In this examination of the temptations of Jesus it is possible to draw a number of conclusions. The first could well be that insufficient attention has been given to them in the past. This is no doubt due to the doctrine that Jesus was without sin, but necessarily implies that He was not a complete human being, like ourselves, a heresy which recognises Him as perfect God, but not perfect man. The true belief must be that He was perfect man during His earthly life and became perfect God because of His resurrection and ascension into heaven.

> 'On the human level he was born of David's stock, but on the level of the spirit – the Holy Spirit – he was declared Son of God by a mighty act in that he rose from the dead.' (Romans 1:4)

To be born of David's stock is to know temptation, to be very human in fact, and that Jesus was so makes his life and teaching wholly effective for us to follow. This is the reason for studying Him in temptation.

In the prayer which Jesus taught His disciples to use there is the petition:

'Do not bring us to the test, but save us from the evil one.'

This is the modern translation as found in the New English Bible, a considerable change from the Authorised Version (the King James Bible) where we find:

'Lead us not into temptation, but deliver us from evil.'

The basic form of the Lord's Prayer is given in Luke (11:2) and there is an expanded version in Matthew (6:9). This means that the basic form at least must have been in 'Q' and have come from the lips of Jesus, and was very likely the way in which He prayed. To be brought to the test is to be compelled to make a decision, and this is where temptation must also be faced. It was in this way that Jesus was tempted and in the final analysis it is in this way that it comes to us all. In the same way, to be saved from the evil one, or delivered from evil, involves making decisions. The making of wise decisions requires all the talent and experience we can muster and, for those of us who are Christians, a firm understanding of the life and teaching of Jesus is the best way to ensure the wisest decision making. We believe that the decisions made by Jesus were in accordance with the Will of His and our heavenly Father. So, again, our aim in facing temptation must be guidance by His example in the sure knowledge that He understood very well what we all have to face. It should therefore be a powerful assistance to us to study His temptations, observe His decisions and so follow Him. This, then, is the principal way in which I hope this book will be of assistance.

We may also conclude that the decisions which Jesus made about the three temptations should guide us in our understanding of those incidents in His ministry which, without that guidance, present great problems. Nor should it be regarded as any lessening of our reverence for Him to have understandable explanations of those incidents. Indeed the reverse should be the case, because otherwise He would appear to have succumbed to temptation.

A third conclusion that could be drawn is that the trials to which Jesus himself referred were substantial, being not only those which derived from the three temptations examined here. There were those arising from relations with His family, which clearly took some time to resolve. He must have regretted having so strongly to challenge the religious establishment, perhaps particularly in the management of the Temple itself, which had originally been His mentor. This in turn aroused the wrath and then the deep enmity of the various groups in that establishment. Finally there were the difficulties He experienced in making His disciples understand the real nature of His mission and the dangers associated with it. Included here is the problem of Judas Iscariot, who was not alone in the way he misunderstood, but certainly was in allowing it to dominate his judgement. In all of these, Jesus must have been tempted to take decisions which would have removed or mitigated these difficulties, but only at the expense of His mission as He understood it.

A fourth conclusion is that the Church at large has neglected the real Jesus as presented by St Mark in favour of the pale image of Him to be found in Matthew and Luke. This arises from the fact that these gospels include the sayings of Jesus which had been preserved in 'Q', together with other important additional material, especially so in the case of Luke. For teaching and preaching these two accordingly have great advantages over Mark, which makes it very important to study what is found only there in order to gain a rounded picture of the man Jesus was.

Then there is Judas Iscariot, 'one of the Twelve' who had followed Jesus from the beginning and seemed to have been a trusted member of that group. My conclusion is that more attention should be given to his story, because he was not a traitor but a misguided follower who thought he knew best.

Had he not destroyed himself, I am sure Jesus would have forgiven him as he forgave Peter, for both men were truly penitent. We would then have been warned by the example of Judas and I think the Church would greatly have profited thereby.

All in all, I think there are good reasons to give careful study to all the matters that have been dealt with in this part of the book.

Part 3

JESUS IN JERUSALEM

An Intellectual Triumph

Introduction

The average Christian, if there is such a person, upon being asked to describe the story of Jesus the Founder of Christianity, would have little difficulty in doing so. He or she would say that Jesus was born in Bethlehem to the Virgin Mary, lived in Nazareth with the Holy Family, was baptised in the River Jordan by John the Baptist and then began His ministry in Palestine, mostly around the Sea of Galilee. Towards the end of that ministry Jesus and His disciples made their way to Jerusalem, where the events of Holy Week took place. A fairly detailed description of these could be given. Apart from this it is unlikely that such a person would expect Jesus to have had any earlier close links with Jerusalem and certainly not with the Jewish establishment there. Yet there are very clear indications in the gospels that this was so, and it could be that Jerusalem and all it stood for had a very considerable influence on Him.

The first indication of this occurs in St Luke, where we are told of the desire of the parents of Jesus immediately after His birth to present Him in the Temple in Jerusalem and do

87

everything that was prescribed in the law of the Lord. Later in that gospel, and in accordance with the same desire, they bring Jesus to the Temple there on His twelfth birthday while they are making their annual visit to Jerusalem for the Passover festival.

A second source is in St Mark's Gospel. Every Christian knows how Jesus was opposed in his preaching and teaching by the Pharisees and doctors of the law who pestered Him with hostile questions. St Mark states that these men came down from Jerusalem, having apparently been sent by the authorities there, and this cannot be without significance since neither Matthew nor Luke includes that information when they refer to these people.

Finally, in St John's Gospel we are told that Jesus made visits to Jerusalem both before and in the course of His ministry and seems to have spent a fair amount of time there. These accounts are evidence that Jesus was well known to the Sanhedrin, the supreme council of the Jews, and make it clear that He was not just a simple Galilean.

The question is whether these contacts with Jerusalem were of any importance to Jesus and had any real effect on His ministry. This Part has been included to show that this must have been so and to explain what may have occurred.

Chapter 16

Jerusalem in St Luke's Gospel

The Background

The first recorded appearance of Jesus in Jerusalem occurs when His parents brought Him there 'to present him to the Lord' (Luke 2:22) in order to comply with the law that 'Every first-born male shall be deemed to belong to the Lord' (v23). 'When they had done everything prescribed in the law of the Lord, they returned to Galilee to their own town of Nazareth' (v39). The birth of Jesus had, of course, taken place in Bethlehem, a few miles south of Jerusalem, and the return journey to Nazareth would have taken Joseph and Mary through the City in any event. Nevertheless their scrupulous observance of the law is full of interest and significance. The fact that it was done is only to be found in St Luke's Gospel and his informant must have been Mary, the Mother of Jesus. Her husband Joseph was the natural father of Jesus, as I have shown in Part One, and was descended from the House of David. Therefore it would be expected that their first son should be born in the city of that great king. That this was so is perhaps the only certain fact we have about the birth of Jesus. It would have been Mary also from whom Luke must have obtained the next account of an occasion when Jesus visited Jerusalem. The latter is preceded by the observation, 'Now it was the practice of his parents to go to Jerusalem every year for the Passover festival' (v41).

It is important to remember what that simple statement must have entailed. Nazareth is some 60 miles north of Jerusalem and the journey from one to the other would almost certainly have had to be made on foot. There were, no doubt, well defined caravan routes, patrolled maybe by the Roman military forces, but probably not without many hazards. For a family with young children, the only safe way would be to travel with friends and neighbours on a journey which was bound to take six or seven days. They would be assisted by donkeys for the carriage of tents, baggage, food and young children and would have to travel at the speed of the slowest member. The size of Joseph's family steadily increased, so that by the time Jesus was 12 there would probably have been three or four more children at least, if not the whole family of seven or more listed by St Mark (6:3). Such seems to have been the situation on the visit made on the occasion when, in accordance with Jewish practice at the time, Jesus came of age and He had to be presented in the temple if that was at all possible (Luke 2:43). A detailed examination will be found in Part One, and I have also reflected briefly there on the possibility that Jesus might have become well known in Jerusalem before He began His ministry. If this was so, it would materially affect our understanding of the circumstances in which that ministry took place. The possibility deserves to be examined in detail.

Conclusions so far

First of all there are some conclusions which I believe can reasonably be drawn from the studies I have already made in this Gospel and these are set out as follows:

1. Jesus was the natural son of Joseph and Mary and a descendant of the House of David.

2. He was an exceptionally gifted child, able at the age of 12 to question the teachers in the Temple at Jerusalem, 'and all who heard him were amazed at his intelligence and the answers he gave' (Luke 2:47).

3. Because of His family's regular annual visits to the City, Jesus must at the age of 12 already have felt quite at home there and had gained the respect of the Temple authorities.

4. In order to be able to bring his family each year to the Festival, Joseph must have been quite successful in his business as a carpenter and builder in Nazareth, so he and his family may have enjoyed a comfortable life style. As for Mary herself, she may well have been like the capable wife described in Proverbs Ch. 31.

Further Deductions

Having laid this foundation, it is possible to consider what further deductions can be made about the connection which Jesus had with Jerusalem. It is reasonable to assume that the annual visits to the Festival would have continued and that His parents would have allowed Jesus to spend time with the teachers in the Temple. On two separate occasions in his Gospel, St Luke comments that Jesus grew big and strong and advanced in favour with God and men (Luke 2:40 and 52). By the time Jesus had reached His twentieth birthday, we could expect to see a commanding presence endowed with wisdom and intelligence of a high order, a Person to take note of even in the teeming crowds at the Passover in Jerusalem itself. He must have become known to a wider circle than the teachers in the Temple and have had acquaintances at least among the Sanhedrin and the Jewish establishment. Apart from that, His family also had their contacts, friends and relations with whom they could stay during the Festival, both in the City and in the nearby villages such as Bethphage, where the disciples found the donkey that would carry Jesus, and Bethany, the home of Martha and Mary.

Thus even before He left Nazareth to prepare for the

ministry it seems very likely that Jesus would not only have been accorded a special status in the synagogue in Nazareth, perhaps even formally a Rabbi there, but would also have been known to the Jewish establishment in Jerusalem. He had perhaps already begun to make His views known there, finding some who were sympathetic to them and realising that there would be quite a strong opposition to any wider expression of them. It was certainly the case that as He moved about in Galilee He was everywhere accorded great respect from the beginning of the ministry, often addressed as Rabbi.

Chapter 17

Jerusalem in St Mark's Gospel

The Visitors from Jerusalem

The contribution in St Mark's Gospel to the links which Jesus had with Jerusalem, apart from Holy Week, is small but nevertheless quite significant. In Part 2, Chapter 9, I have shown how the true Jesus is only found in this Gospel, although it provides the basic account for both Matthew and Luke. These two make many omissions, as I have made clear, and another of these relates to those lawyers and others who were continually questioning Jesus, often in a hostile fashion. The other two Gospels refer to the questioners only as doctors of the law, Pharisees, etc, but St Mark explains that 'they had come down from Jerusalem'. He does not say why they had done so, though as their motives are made quite clear there was no need. They wanted to break down the hold which Jesus had over the people by trying to show Him at fault. They were doing this because they were strongly representative of the powers that be in Jerusalem, who were highly suspicious of Jesus and aware of the leadership that he was establishing. They could not accept His liberalisation of the law of Moses and were becoming more and more concerned that their position was being undermined. So we find quite early on in this Gospel that 'the Pharisees ... began plotting against him ... to see how they could make away with him' (Mark 3:6). For this to have happened at the outset of the ministry must have implied some knowledge in Jerusalem of the kind of person Jesus was and the sort of views He held, with consequent fears about what He was doing.

Their Hostility Revealed

Why then was it that in a well-known incident Matthew and Luke omit the reference to Jerusalem? Mark tells how the doctors of the law who had come down from Jerusalem said of Jesus 'He is possessed by Beelzebub ... and drives out devils by the prince of devils' (Mark 3:22). In the parallel passage in Matthew, after Jesus had cured a blind and dumb man, the result is that 'the Pharisees ... said "It is only by Beelzebub ... that this man drives the devils out".' (Matthew 12:24). Similarly in Luke, it is some of the people who make this comment (Luke 11:15). Luke does not otherwise imply any hostility to Jesus from the people yet at the end of the same chapter he tells how 'the lawyers and Pharisees began to assail him fiercely and to ply him with a host of questions, laying snares to catch him with his own words' (Luke 11:53,54). From where would these people have come if not from Jerusalem, and surely they must have known Jesus and been familiar with His views in order to have turned upon Him in this way so early in His public ministry?

These two Gospels were produced some 10 to 15 years later than that of Mark, and the Early Church would have had goodly numbers of Jewish Christians, perhaps especially so in or near Jerusalem. This may have been the reason for Matthew and Luke, writing quite independently of each other, to have played down the hostility to Jesus of the Jewish leaders in Jerusalem. The situation had certainly changed some 15 or 20 years later, when St John's Gospel was produced, for that emphasises very strongly the enmity of the Jews in Jerusalem.

Chapter 18

Jerusalem in St John's Gospel

The Historical Accuracy of this Gospel

From the accounts of the public ministry of Jesus as it is described in the three synoptic gospels, it would not appear that He visited Jerusalem until the final Passover Festival in what Christians know as Holy Week. This does, in fact, seem unlikely in view of all the contacts He had there. Thus it is not at all surprising that St John in his Gospel tells of other occasions when Jesus was in Jerusalem and these are worthy of careful examination. Although this Gospel is very different from the others, it is the only one whose author was a disciple of Jesus and moreover the one who was His closest friend. This John was most probably not the person who actually wrote the Gospel, but most scholars now regard him as the author who dictated his account when an old man to his own disciple, known as John the Elder. The latter would have had no hesitation in describing his mentor in the Gospel as 'the disciple whom Jesus loved' as a good way of identifying him. A scribe in these circumstances, listening to the author, might easily confuse the latter's own words with his recollection of the words of Jesus, as indeed has happened. He would,

95

however, have his own knowledge of places visited by Jesus and would have a clearer understanding of His actions. In this sense, increasing reliance is being placed on the historical accuracy of St John's gospel. We can therefore turn with confidence to the accounts of the visits referred to above.

The Testimony of John the Baptist

It is of interest to note how at the outset of this Gospel great interest is taken by the Jewish hierarchy in what was going on in the country areas of what we now know as Palestine. In Chapter 1, v19, we read that 'the Jews of Jerusalem sent a deputation of priests and Levites to ask (John the Baptist) who he was.' From this it is clear that the term 'Jews of Jerusalem' really means the leaders of the people, because only they could have sent such a deputation. Moreover, the ordinary folk would hardly have been capable of carrying on the technical discussions which the members of the deputation had first with the Baptist and later with Jesus, which John records. The Baptist, according to this account, tells them that among them, though they do not know him, 'stands the one who is to come after me. I am not good enough to unfasten his shoes' (v28). When this was reported back, it is no wonder that as soon as the news reached Jerusalem of the appearance of Jesus preaching and teaching in Galilee, a similar deputation would be sent to question Him.

The First Visit and the Meeting with Nicodemus

The first of the visits which Jesus made to Jerusalem occurs very early (John 2:12): 'As it was near the time of the Jewish Passover, Jesus went up to Jerusalem.' It had, of course, been His custom to do so, though it does not seem that on this occasion He was accompanied by His family, who, having visited Him in Capernaum, had returned to Nazareth. There follows a description of the cleansing of the Temple, an event which the other gospels place in Holy Week, which seems a much more likely time for it. St John's custom was to use special events as signs and he uses the cleansing here, before the public ministry had begun, to demonstrate the power that Jesus could and did exercise over all kinds of people. He also reports that many wanted to give their allegiance to Jesus, but as He had not yet opened His mission, He did not encourage them at this stage. There then follows the famous account of the visit of Nicodemus, 'a member of the Jewish Council, who came to Jesus by night. "Rabbi," he said, "we know that you are a teacher sent by God".' (John 3:1,2). John describes the conversation in which Jesus explains the need for those who wish to see the kingdom of God to be born again. This account is a clear example of how the writer, John the Elder, could not tell when the author's account of the words of Jesus ends and his own reflections thereon begin. Indeed no one can, thus not making a clear distinction between writer and author. It is, however, the fact of this visit and the opening observation of Nicodemus that now calls for study.

The Jewish council, of which Nicodemus was a member, was the Sanhedrin. Although primarily a religious body, it was recognised by the Roman power as having great authority among the Jews. As has already been suggested above, the emergence of Jesus as a person of singular distinction must have come to the notice of the Sanhedrin. When Nicodemus arrived, John, the beloved disciple, must have been with Jesus and since he 'was acquainted with the High Priest' (John 18:15) may well have been acquainted also with Nicodemus and may have effected an introduction. On the other hand there is the possibility that Jesus had already met Nicodemus at meetings in the Temple. Thus the form of address which Nicodemus uses is most interesting, indicating that this distinguished Jew acknowledges the status of Jesus, calling Him Rabbi. Then he says 'We know', presumably speaking on behalf of other members of the Sanhedrin as well as himself, 'that you are a teacher sent by God'.

Jesus Known to the Sanhedrin

Because of the way in which St John's Gospel is constructed, it is difficult to relate its timing of events to those that are recorded in the other gospels. It would seem, however, that the incident we are considering took place before Jesus had opened His public ministry in Galilee. Yet His regular annual, and perhaps even more frequent, visits to Jerusalem in the past have clearly already convinced at least some of the leading figures there that He was a unique figure 'sent by God'. These were a minority of the Council, who felt they could not express their views openly, so Nicodemus had to make a clandestine visit to Jesus by night. From now on in St John's gospel we find that Jesus is in Jerusalem on several occasions and, because of the explanations given above, there can be no reason to doubt that this was so. It is noticeable that the Gospel's accounts reveal a good knowledge of the city and can be regarded as wholly reliable.

Return to Galilee

There is no knowing how long the 'Nicodemus' visit lasted, probably only for the duration of the festival, as would most likely have been the normal custom of Joseph's family. At Chapter 3, v22, we learn that on leaving the City Jesus went to Aenon, near to Salim in North Judea, and in Chapter 4 He sets out for Galilee. On arrival there He is welcomed by the Galileans 'because they had seen all that he did at the festival in Jerusalem; they had been at the festival themselves' (v45). Here we have a quite different link with that City and it would not have been only the Galileans who saw Jesus there. St Mark records that 'Great numbers from Galilee, Judea and Jerusalem, Idumaea and Transjordan and the neighbourhood of Tyre and Sidon heard what he was doing and came to see him' (3:7). They must have come, in effect, from every area which maintained the Jewish tradition and particularly the connection with Jerusalem. Thus the very early success of the public ministry in Galilee may well have stemmed from the fact that the people had already come to know Jesus in Jerusalem.

Second and Third Visits – the Arrest of Jesus Ordered

The Gospel now continues with the next occasion when Jesus is found in the City. Chapter 5 begins with a visit 'for one of the Jewish festivals' and a detailed description follows of the cure at the Sheep-Pool on the Sabbath of 'a man who had been crippled for thirty-eight years.' John goes on to record that, 'It was works of this kind done on the Sabbath that stirred the Jews to persecute Jesus.' In Chapter 6 Jesus is back in Galilee, where He had withdrawn to the farther shore of the Sea of Galilee, where John sets the feeding of the five thousand. In Chapter 7 (3,10) we find Jesus again in Jerusalem at the Feast of Tabernacles; He is teaching in the Temple and already many of the people have begun to believe in him. 'When the Messiah comes,' they said, 'is it likely that he will perform more signs than this man?' (v31). The temple police are accordingly instructed to arrest Him, but they report back to the chief priests and Pharisees without Jesus and explain, 'No man ever spoke as this man speaks'(v46). They are angrily denounced, and this gives Nicodemus an opportunity to make a defence. 'Does our law,' he asked them, 'permit us to pass judgment on a man unless we have first given him a hearing and learned the facts?' He is promptly accused of being a Galilean and of not knowing that prophets do not come from Galilee. On such slender grounds the Sanhedrin is apparently prepared to base its case against the Son of Man.

We cannot tell how long Jesus remained in Jerusalem, but on this occasion He may have stayed on for a little time after the end of the Feast. During it He cured, on a Sabbath day, the man who had been blind from his birth and who was brought before the Pharisees to explain why this had occurred. The story is told at length in Chapter 9 and leads on in the next chapter to a demand from the Jews (? their leaders as above) 'How long must you keep us in suspense? If you are the Messiah say so plainly' (10:24). Jesus refuses to give them a plain answer because He will not accept the political implications of their understanding of that term. Instead, according to this Gospel, He infuriates them by His claim to be 'acting as my Father would' and that they should accept the evidence of His deeds (10:27). He then withdrew across the Jordan and did not again enter Jerusalem until the events of Holy Week.

Chapter 19

Further Conclusions

From this brief study of these three Gospels, it is plain that Jesus had very real and close links with Jerusalem all his life. Does this make any great difference to our understanding of Him? There can be no question but that He was essentially a Galilean, a Nazarene, since He was often hailed as Jesus of Nazareth. His public ministry, too, largely took place in the country and not in Jerusalem, though it must have been strongly influenced by His connections with, and visits to, that City. It must therefore be of importance to realise what those connections were and the degree of influence they had.

Jesus Officially Recognised in Jerusalem

First of all, it seems absolutely clear that Jesus held an official position within the Jewish religious establishment. This is recognised by Nicodemus in addressing Him as 'Rabbi', and even going so far as to say that members of the Sanhedrin of his way of thinking regarded Jesus as having been 'sent by God'. This was before the public ministry had commenced and must therefore have been based on their knowledge of Jesus resulting from His annual visits, with His family, to the Passover festivals. If the teachers in the Temple, and all who heard Him, 'were amazed at his intelligence and the answers he gave' (Luke 2:47) when He was only 12, they must have watched His progress year by year with the most profound astonishment. Everyone must indeed have realised that the only explanation was that here indeed was a man 'sent by God'. It is very likely that in Jerusalem Jesus would have been held in honour, have had open access to the Temple and many friends among the rulers of the people. There may already have been many messianic hopes pinned upon Him, so that He may have been compelled to reveal something of the way His thoughts were developing, which would not have been well accepted by the leaders of the Jews. When Nicodemus came to Him at night he must have indicated a coolness towards Jesus amongst his colleagues and might have wished to act as an honest broker, to use a modern term. Jesus, of course, would have none of it, demanding instead the radical change of a new birth.

Thus it came about that, when Jesus began His ministry, a deputation was sent from Jerusalem to keep watch upon Him.

A Rabbi in Nazareth

Secondly, a special situation must have developed in Nazareth, as I have already shown in Part One. The people there could not have been other than proud of Jesus because of what He was and the reputation He had gained in Jerusalem. If He was a Rabbi there, He must certainly have been so in Nazareth, and the references in the gospels to the visit He made there during the ministry make this clear. In His home town, however, Jesus was also the carpenter and builder and a member of a sizeable family. So the local view of His excellence would have had as much to do with His business and social activities as with His position in the synagogue. In due course He ruefully admitted that 'a prophet will always be held in honour except in his home town and among his kinsmen and family' (Mark 6:4).

102

Jesus no Galilean Peasant

The final conclusion is that Jesus was no Galilean peasant, who suddenly emerged to astonish the Jewish people. He was instead an acknowledged descendant of the House of David, a man honoured in Jerusalem, living comfortably in Nazareth, where He also was held in great esteem. His decision to embark upon a public ministry which demanded such radical changes in the observances of the Mosaic law, and the rabbinical rules developed from it, must have sent shock waves throughout the entire Jewish community and not least in Jerusalem. The effect of them continues still.

The conclusions noted above make it clear that Jesus was well known in Jerusalem long before He began His public ministry. This must have been a factor which made it very necessary for Him to avoid the title of 'Messiah' or 'King of the Jews', because of the political implications they contained. On the other hand, the immediate success He achieved inevitably brought these titles into prominence, even among His own disciples. Only His devotion to the Will of His heavenly Father and the constant presence of the Holy Spirit enabled Jesus to carry on His mission for as long as He did. In the end, however, it was the political factor that was the excuse for His crucifixion.

Part 4

'Q'

A Possible Reconstruction

Introduction – What is 'Q'?

St Luke in his Gospel, and the writers of the Gospel attributed to St Matthew, made copious use of that composed by St Mark, believed to be the earliest of the four gospels to appear. It seems very likely that the two former Gospels also used another document, of which copies had circulated before St Mark's Gospel had been written. The existence of such a document was first proposed by biblical scholars in Germany, who named it 'Quelle', source, though it is now generally referred to as 'Q'. It appears to have been an *aide mémoire* consisting of important sayings of Jesus and does not include any historical narrative nor any reference to the events of Holy Week. It is hardly surprising, therefore, that when its material had been incorporated in Matthew and Luke there was no longer any reason to maintain its separate existence. At that time, the copying of documents was a long and laborious task and St Mark may well not have included 'Q' in his Gospel because of this, and in order to shorten that task in his case.

Thus, although there is no surviving copy of 'Q', the material it contained which was used in Matthew and Luke can be found by comparing the two texts. In spite of the vicissitudes of copying, printing, translating, editing, etc, which these texts have experienced, it is still possible to isolate extracts which could have come from 'Q'. Twelve can be found where the words used are identical and a further six where the similarities are so close as to indicate a common source. I have always thought it strange that, as it is reasonably possible to do this and let the result be known to the Church, it appears never to have been done in any popular form. 'Q' has the immense interest of being the Christian document closest to the time of Jesus and must represent what whoever produced it thought were the most important sayings of His. Moreover, these sayings are more likely to be the *ipsissima verba* of Jesus, his very own words, than any others to be found in the gospels. The compiler would almost certainly have to have been one of the disciples. St Matthew himself has been suggested and indeed, as a tax gatherer, he must have been able to keep records.

Naturally there are variations in what is found in the two Gospels, but it is the general agreement between them that would confirm the existence of a separate document. There is now the opportunity to make 'Q' available and extracts that can be identified are set out below in the order in which they appear in Matthew. Where introductory or linking words are needed, these have generally been taken from Matthew's Gospel. This is because Luke is more likely to have edited or extended the text than is the case with the writers of Matthew. This might be additional evidence for regarding this disciple as the compiler of 'Q' and thus for naming the Gospel after him.

In the following reconstruction of 'Q' the extracts from the Gospels of Matthew and Luke are taken from the *New English Bible*, as are the other biblical quotations in this book. In Section A of the Sayings the texts printed in bold type are taken from Matthew and are the same words used in the same order as in Luke. The words in small type are found only in Matthew and those in brackets are found only in Luke. Headings and other added notes are in italics.

The Sayings of Jesus as they might have been found in 'Q'

A   Uniform or Nearly Uniform Texts in Matthew and Luke

1   Temptations. Belief and Trust in God
Jesus was led away by the Spirit into the wilderness and tempted by the devil. For forty days he fasted and at the end of them he was famished. The tempter said to him 'If you are the Son of God tell these stones to become bread'. Jesus answered 'Scripture says "Man cannot live on bread alone". The devil took him to Jerusalem and set him on the parapet of the temple. 'If you are the Son of God' he said 'Throw yourself down, for Scripture says "He will put his angels in charge of you and they will support you in their arms for fear you should strike your foot against a stone." Jesus answered him 'Scripture says again "You are not to put the Lord your God to the test".' The devil showed him all the kingdoms of the world. 'All these' he said 'I will give you if you will only do me homage' Jesus said 'Scripture says "You shall

do homage to the Lord your God and worship him alone".'

Matt 4:1–10 Luke 4:1–12

Note: The temptations are in the order given in Matthew.

2   *Beatitudes. How blest is Humility and Steadfastness*
He said to his disciples

How blest are those who know their need of God the kingdom of Heaven (God) is theirs
How blest are those who hunger they shall be satisfied
How blest are the sorrowful (You who weep now) they shall find consolation (You shall laugh)
How blest are you when you suffer insults and persecution for my sake (you are when they outlaw you and ban your name because of the Son of Man) Accept it with gladness and exultation (Be glad and dance for joy) for you have a rich reward in heaven, in the same way they persecuted (did their fathers treat) the prophets

Matt 5:1,3,4,6 and 10–12 Luke 6:20–2

3   *The Lord's Prayer*
This is how you should pray: (when you pray say:)

Father, thy name be hallowed
Thy kingdom come
Give us today (each day) our daily bread
Forgive us the wrong we have done (our sins)
As we have forgiven those who have wronged us
(For we too forgive all who have done us wrong)
And do not bring us to the test

Matt 6:9–13 Luke 11:2–4

4   *Persistence in Prayer*
Ask and you will receive
Knock and the door will be opened
For everyone who asks receives
He who seeks finds
And to him who knocks the door will be opened
Is there a man (father) among you who will offer his son a snake when he asks for fish
If you then bad as you are know how to give your children what is good for them
How much more will your (the) heavenly Father give good things (the Holy Spirit) to those who ask him!

Matt 7:7–11 Luke 11:9–13

5   *The Centurion's Servant – Faith Rewarded*
He went to (entered) **Capernaum** and a centurion asked for his help because a boy of his (valued servant) was very ill. Jesus said 'I will come and cure him', but the centurion replied 'Sir, who am I to have you under my roof. Say the word and the boy (servant) will be cured. I know for I am myself under orders with soldiers under me. I say to one "Go" and he goes, to another "Come here" and he comes and to my servant "Do this" and he does it' Jesus heard him with astonishment and said to the people who were following him 'I tell you this nowhere even in Israel have I found such faith'. Jesus said to the centurion 'Because of your faith so let it be'. At that moment the boy (servant) recovered.

Matt 8:5–13 Luke 7:1–10

Note: Luke has the centurion send Jewish elders as messengers to Jesus and makes appropriate changes.

6   *Discipleship   Follow Jesus First*
A doctor of the law (man) **said 'I will follow you wherever you**

go' Jesus replied (answered) 'Foxes have their holes, the birds their roosts, but the Son of Man has nowhere to lay his head' Another said 'Lord, let me go and bury my father first' Jesus replied (said) 'Follow me, leave the dead to bury their dead'

Matt 8:19–22 Luke 10:13 and 14

7 *John the Baptist   The Great Herald of Jesus*

John sent his disciples to Christ (the Lord) with this message 'Are you the one who is to come or are we to expect some other?' Jesus answered 'Go and tell John what you hear and see, the blind recover their sight, the lame walk, the lepers are made clean, the deaf hear, the dead are raised to life, the poor are hearing the good news and happy is the man who does not find me a stumbling block.' When the messengers had left Jesus began to speak to the people (crowds) about John. 'What was the spectacle that drew you to the wilderness? A reed bed swept by the wind? No? Then what did you go out to see? A man dressed in silks and satins? Surely you must look in palaces for that (grand clothes and luxury). But why did you go out? To see a prophet? (What did you go out to see? A prophet?) Yes indeed and far more than a prophet. He is the man of whom Scripture says:

"Here is my herald, whom I send on ahead of you and he will prepare your way before you."

I tell you never has there appeared on earth a mother's son (there is not a mother's son) greater than John and yet the least in the kingdom of Heaven (God) is greater than he.
How can I describe (the people of) this generation. They are like children sitting in the market place and shouting at each other:

'Q'

We piped for you and you would not dance
We wept and wailed and you would not mourn.

For John came neither eating nor drinking and they say "He is possessed!" the Son of Man came eating and drinking and they say "Look at him! A glutton and a drinker, a friend of tax-gatherers and sinners!" And yet God's wisdom is proved right by its results (all who are his children).'

Matt 11:2–11 and 16-19 Luke 7:19–28 and ???

8   The Unrepentant Cities of North Galilee
Alas for you Chorazim! Alas for you Bethsaida! If the miracles that were performed in you had been performed in Tyre and Sidon they would have repented long ago in sackcloth and ashes. But it will be more bearable for Tyre and Sidon on the day of (at the) Judgement than for you.

Matt 11:21,22 Luke 10:13,14

9   Revelation
I thank thee Father, Lord of heaven and earth, for hiding these things from the learned and wise and revealing them to the simple. Yes, Father, such was thy choice. Everything is entrusted to me by my Father and no one knows the Son (who the Son is) but the Father and no one knows the Father (or who the Father is) but the Son and those to whom the Son may choose to reveal him.

Matt 11:25–27 Luke 10:21,22

10   The Kingdom of God Prevails over Beelzebub
Jesus drives out a devil and the people said:
'It is by Beelzebub prince of devils that this man drives the devils out!' He knew what was in their minds so he said 'Every kingdom divided against itself goes to ruin, no house-

hold divided against itself can stand (and a divided household falls). If Satan is divided against himself, how can his kingdom stand? If it is by Beelzebub that I cast out devils. By whom do your own people drive them out? If this is your argument they themselves will refute you. But if it is by the Spirit (finger) of God that I drive out the devils, then be sure the kingdom of God has already come upon you.'

Matt 12:24–28 Luke 11:15–20

11 *Jerusalem. The Faithless City*

O Jerusalem, Jerusalem, the city that murders the prophets and stones the messengers sent to her! How often have I longed to gather your children as a hen gathers her brood under her wings, but you would not let me. Look! Look! there is your temple, forsaken by God. And I tell you, you shall never see me until the time when you say 'Blessings on him who comes in the name of the Lord'

Matt 23:37–39 Luke 13:34,35

12 *The Trusty Servant*

Remember, if the householder had known at what time the burglar was coming he would not have let his house be broken into. Hold yourselves ready therefore because the Son of Man will come at the time you least expect him. Who is the trusty servant, the sensible man charged by his master to manage his household staff (and sensible man whom his master will appoint as his steward to manage his servants) and issue their rations at the proper time? Happy that servant who is found at his task when his master comes! I tell you this: he will be put in charge of all his master's property. But if he (that servant) says to himself 'The master is a long time coming' and begins to bully the other servants (menservants and maids) and eat and drink with his drunken friends (get drunk) then the master will arrive on a day that servant does not expect at a time he does not know and will cut him in pieces. Thus he will find his place among the hypocrites (faithless).

Matt 24:43–51 Luke 12:39–46

B   Texts with Great Similarities

In addition to the extracts 1–12 above, there are the following five which have such great similarities that they must also have been derived from 'Q'.

13   Reconciliation

If some one sues you, come to terms with him promptly while you are both on your way to court; otherwise he may hand you over to the judge, and the judge to the constable and you will be put in jail. I tell you, once you are there you will not be let out till you have paid the last farthing.

Matt 5:25,26

When you are going with your opponent to court, make an effort to settle with him while you are still on the way; otherwise he may drag you before the judge and the judge hand you over to the constable and the constable put you in jail. I tell you, you will not come out till you have paid the last farthing.

Luke 12:58,59

14   The Lost Sheep

Suppose a man has a hundred sheep. If one of them strays does he not leave the other ninety-nine on the hillside and go in search of the one that strayed? And if he should find it I tell you this, he is more delighted over that sheep than over the ninety-nine that never strayed.

Matt 18:12–14

If one of you has a hundred sheep and loses one of them does he not leave the ninety-nine in the open pasture and go after the missing one until he has found it? How delighted he is then! He lifts it on to his shoulders and home he goes to call his friends and neighbours together. 'Rejoice with me' he cries 'I have found my lost sheep'. In the same way I tell you there will be greater joy in heaven over one sinner who repents than over ninety-nine righteous people who do not need to repent.

Luke 15:4–7

15 Forgiveness
Peter asked him 'Lord, how often am I to forgive my brother if he goes on wronging me? As many as seven times?' Jesus replied 'I do not say seven times, I say seventy times seven'.

Matt 18:21,22

If your brother wrongs you, reprove him and if he repents forgive him. Even if he wrongs you seven times in a day and comes back to you seven times saying 'I am sorry' you are to forgive him.

Luke 17:3,4

16 Where to seek Treasure
Do not store up for yourselves treasure on earth where it grows rusty and moth-eaten and thieves break in to steal it. Store up treasure in heaven where there is no moth and no rust to spoil it, no thieves to break in and steal. For where your treasure is there will your heart be also.

Matt 6:19–21

Sell your possessions and give in charity. Provide for yourselves purses that do not wear out and never failing treasure in heaven where no thief can get near it, no moth destroy it. For where your treasure is there will your heart be also.

Luke 12:33,34

17   The Family Divided

You must not think that I have come to bring peace to the earth, but a sword. I have come to set a man against his father, a daughter against her mother, a son's wife against her mother-in-law.

Matt 10:34,35

Do you suppose I came to establish peace on earth? No, indeed, I have come to bring division. From now on members of a family will be divided, father against son, mother against daughter, son's wife against her mother-in-law.

Luke 12:51–53

C   A Parable with a Common Origin

18

The parable of the talents, or bags of gold, in Matt 25:14–30 is paralleled by that of the pounds in Luke 19:11–28, though the ways in which the story is told differ considerably. Nevertheless the parable would appear to have a common origin in 'Q'. The context is certainly one that might have been of particular interest to Matthew!

Appendix

Judas, Son of Simon Iscariot
A New Look

The Gospel Accounts

The behaviour of Judas Iscariot is the great enigma of the
Christian tradition and, since it plays so important a part in
the temptations of Jesus, I think it is not inappropriate to give
it some special consideration.

In the references to the betrayal of Jesus by Judas to be
found in the synoptic gospels, he is almost always referred to
as 'one of the Twelve'. These were the men who were chosen
by Jesus at the very outset of His ministry and St John records
that He said, 'Have I not chosen you, all twelve?' (John 6:70).
We do not know what process of selection Jesus used, but it is
clear that there were those among His followers who were
not selected and yet remained very close to Him. We have
only to remember Joseph Barsabbas Justus and Matthias,
who were candidates to fill the vacancy caused by the death
of Judas. Their qualification was that they were 'one of those
who bore us company all the while we had the Lord Jesus
with us', as St Peter announced to the assembled brotherhood
(Acts 1:21). St Luke describes how Jesus 'appointed a further

117

seventy two and sent them on ahead in pairs to every town and place he was going to visit himself' (Luke 10:1). The Twelve were therefore a very special group which included the closest friends of Jesus as well as those who may have had some special background. Among them it may be significant to note that there are three instances where the name of a father is given. The best known of these will be Zebedee, the father of James and John, who must have been well known as the proprietor of a fishery business on the Sea of Galilee. This circumstance might be deduced from the fact that when Jesus called his two sons they went off 'leaving their father Zebedee in the boat with the hired men' (Mark 1:20). In the parallel case of Simon and Andrew, 'they left their nets and followed him,' so Zebedee was worthy of mention. Then in all three lists of the disciples as appointed by Jesus, there is a second James, who is the son of Alphaeus, though this may only have been noted to distinguish him from the other James. Finally, St John records that Judas was the son of Simon Iscariot (6:70), perhaps implying that Simon was a man of some importance, like Zebedee.

In considering the status of Judas it may be noted that in St Matthew's version of the betrayal Jesus says to Judas, 'Friend, do what you are here to do' (Matt 26:50), which must indicate that Jesus had some idea of what Judas then intended. Yet it can hardly be supposed that Judas had revealed any defect that even Jesus could be aware of at the time he was chosen. There is one other singular fact about Judas made known by St John: 'Judas was in charge of the common purse' (John 13:29). No other disciple had a par-ticular role so far as we know, though Peter may have been a spokesman for them. We do not know if Jesus had invited Judas to take on the work of treasurer for the group of people who followed Him or whether it just came about, but it would seem he had been accepted by them all. This might have been an expression of confidence in him and the duties it involved may have had that wider significance which the managing of money on behalf of others almost necessarily entails. Thus, at the Last Supper, the verse in St John's gospel quoted above goes on, 'Some supposed that ... Jesus was telling him to buy what was needed for the festival, or to make some gift to the poor.' It may well have been the case that Judas was a sort of general manager for what had become quite a large company of those who followed Jesus. The extraordinary thing is that a man who must have enjoyed this special role, and felt that he was playing a helpful part in the enormous success that Jesus was currently experiencing in Jerusalem, should have wanted to bring about the death of Jesus or to be in any way involved in such a catastrophe. It is not surprising to read in St Matthew his agonised confession: ' "I have sinned," he said, "I have brought an innocent man to his death," and he went and hanged himself' (Matt 27:4). What, then, made him do it?

Before considering the matter any further, we should first read the account which each of the Evangelists has given of what Judas did. The earliest is of course that of St Mark:

'Then Judas Iscariot, one of the Twelve, went to the chief priests to betray him to them. When they heard what he had come for, they were greatly pleased and promised him money; and he began to look for a good opportunity to betray him' (14:10). Such is the plot; next follows the arrest of Jesus:

'The third time he [Jesus] came and said to them "Still sleeping? Still taking your ease? Enough! The hour has come. The Son of Man is betrayed to sinful men. Up, let us go forward! My betrayer is upon us." Suddenly, while he was still speaking, Judas, one of the Twelve, appeared and with him was a crowd armed with swords and cudgels, sent by the chief priests, lawyers and elders. Now the traitor had agreed with them upon a signal: "The one I kiss is your man; seize him and get him safely away." When he reached the spot, he stepped forward at once and said to Jesus, "Rabbi" and kissed him. They then seized him and held him fast' (14:43–46).

The account in St Matthew, probably written some 20 years later and based on Mark, has some changes in its story of the plot:

'Then one of the Twelve, the man called Judas Iscariot, went to the chief priests and said, "What will you give me to betray him to you?" They weighed him out thirty silver pieces. From that moment he began to look for a good opportunity to betray him' (Matt 26:14–16).

The account of the arrest begins with the same words of Jesus as in Mark and continues: 'While he was still speaking, Judas, one of the Twelve, appeared; with him was a great crowd armed with swords and cudgels, sent by the chief priests and the elders of the nation. The traitor gave them this sign: "The one I kiss is your man; seize him"; and stepping forward at once he said "Hail, Rabbi!" and kissed him. Jesus replied, "Friend, do what you are here to do." They then came forward, seized Jesus and held him fast' (Matt 26:47–50).

Matthew now concludes the story:

'When Judas the traitor saw that Jesus had been condemned, he was seized with remorse and returned the thirty silver pieces to the chief priests and elders. "I have sinned," he said; "I have brought an innocent man to his death." But they said, "What is that to us? See to that yourself." So he threw the money down in the temple and left them, and went and hanged himself' (Matt 27:3–5).

In verses 6–10, Matthew tells how the chief priests used the money to buy a field which became known as 'Blood Acre', giving fulfilment to the prophecy of Jeremiah that thirty pieces of silver, the price set on his head, should be so used, though the prophecy is actually in Zech 11:13.

Luke's account, contemporary, it is thought, with that of Matthew, describes the plot in a slightly different way:

'Then Satan entered into Judas Iscariot, who was one of the Twelve; and Judas went to the chief priests and officers of the temple police to discuss ways and means of putting Jesus into their power. They were greatly pleased and undertook to pay him a sum of money. He agreed and began to look out for an opportunity to betray him to them without collecting a crowd' (Luke 22:3–6). The arrest is very briefly described:

'While he was still speaking a crowd appeared with the man called Judas, one of the Twelve, at their head. He came up to Jesus to kiss him; but Jesus said, "Judas, would you betray the Son of Man with a kiss?" (Luke 22:47,48).

Also, in the Acts of the Apostles, Luke has this note:

'This Judas, be it noted, after buying a plot of land with the price of his villainy, fell forward on the ground and burst open so that his entrails poured out. This became known to everyone in Jerusalem and they named the property ... "Blood Acre"' (Acts 1:18,19).

John, written later still, does not record the details of the plot, but this is his account of the arrest:

'Jesus went out with his disciples and crossed the Kedron ravine. There was a garden there and he and his disciples went into it. The place was known to Judas, his betrayer, because Jesus had often met there with his disciples. So Judas took a detachment of soldiers and police provided by the chief priests and the Pharisees, equipped with lanterns, torches and weapons, and made his way to the garden. Jesus, knowing all that was coming upon him, went out to them and asked, "Who is it you want?" "Jesus of Nazareth," they answered. Jesus said, "I am he." And there stood Judas the traitor with them' (John 18:1–5).

A Study of These Accounts

Several points emerge from these extracts. In each of their references to Judas in describing the plot and the arrest, Matthew, Mark and Luke all refer to him as 'one of the Twelve'; John also, when he first refers to Judas, uses the same term, a description applied only to him. This must mean that the disciples had no idea of what Judas was planning and were horrified that a hitherto trusted disciple should behave as he did. The 30 pieces of silver is clearly an elaboration by Matthew in accord with his practice of endeavouring to locate a suitable Old Testament prophecy for any important event. The combined list of the Jewish establishment who were involved in the plot with Judas, or in the arrest of Jesus, is astonishingly all-embracing: the chief priests, officers of the temple police, lawyers, elders of the nation and the Pharisees are all to be found. The chief priests are the only group named by all the Evangelists, but the Early Church no doubt regarded all the others as implicated and indeed this might well have been necessary in order to secure such speedy action. In John's account of the arrest, Jesus, completely aware of the position, identifies Himself to the soldiers and temple police, believing it to be the Will of His Father, and Judas plays no part except to bring them to the Garden. Finally, there is Matthew's account of the remorse and suicide of Judas, which confirms that it was in no way his intention to encompass the death of Jesus.

The great temptation for managers is that they may believe they know best what needs to be done and that they must overrule the specialists who do not have management skills. Judas may have felt that he understood the ways of the world better than even Jesus Himself. He probably thought that the great success and popularity which Jesus had achieved with the common people in Jerusalem needed to be exploited and Judas seems to have tried to persuade Jesus to confront the chief priests and rulers on behalf of the people. He must have seen with awe how Jesus had taken possession, as it were, of the Temple precincts and thought that the exploitation of this should be the line of action. Jesus would at once have realised that it would have meant falling into the third temptation, the seeking after worldly power, and rejected such advice. Judas, however, thought he knew best and seems to have determined to force the hand of Jesus by organising a confrontation in which he was certain Jesus would triumph, though it would necessitate Jesus first being placed in the power of his enemies.

In his knowledge of the ways of the world, Judas was no match for the chief priests and those who worked with them. They had already made their plan, which was to arrest Jesus at night when He would have no protection from the people and then to bring about His death in the shortest possible time before the Sabbath; and immediately before the Passover gave a special opportunity. There would not then be the possibility for His friends to rally support for Him, but the problem would be to identify Jesus in the darkness. One of them could have been present to do this, but then Judas comes to tell them of his plan which fitted in so well with their own. It would not have occurred to Judas that the chief priests could organise so speedy a trial and immediate execution. So his desire to see the triumph of Jesus, as we must suppose, made Judas a willing tool to help bring about His death.

It seems to me, therefore, that we should understand the behaviour of Judas and take warning from it. He was a betrayer, because he failed to follow Jesus, a guilt which we all share, but he was not a simple traitor and it is wrong to ignore his story for that reason.

Part One of this book has been separately
published as a booklet, *Jesus in Nazareth and Capernaum*;
ISBN 1 85977 070 3. Copies may be obtained from the
publisher, price £2.50.